Robinson
Crusoe

Chosen Classics, Abridged

DANIEL DEFOE

Robinson Crusoe

WEBSTER'S WORD POWER ENGLISH READERS

With Audiobook, Notes and Glossary

Published 2016 by Geddes & Grosset, an imprint of
The Gresham Publishing Company Ltd, Academy Park,
Building 4000, Gower Street, Glasgow, G51 1PR, Scotland.

www.geddesandgrosset.com
Contact us at info@geddesandgrosset.com
Find us on ⓕ facebook/pages/geddesandgrosset

The publisher acknowledges support from Creative
Scotland towards the publication of this title.

ALBA | CHRUTHACHAIL

ISBN 978 1 910965 32 0

Printed and bound in India.

Contents

Introduction

To the Reader

When the novel *Robinson Crusoe* was first published in 1719, many people believed that the title character, Robinson Crusoe, was a real person. They thought that the novel was his autobiography and that it contained a true description of the years he spent as a castaway on a remote tropical island. The real writer of Robinson Crusoe's exciting tale was, in fact, Daniel Defoe (1660–1731).

However, few readers could have missed the resemblance of Defoe's main character, Robinson Crusoe, to Alexander Selkirk, a Scottish sailor who really did spend more than four years as a castaway after being marooned on an uninhabited island in the South Pacific Ocean. By the time Selkirk was rescued, he had become adept at hunting and making use of the resources he found on the island. His story of survival was widely publicized when he returned home and it became a likely source (but probably not the only source) of inspiration for the writer Daniel Defoe's fictional character, Robinson Crusoe.

The twists and turns in the life of Defoe's main character give us plenty of surprises as well as a convincing picture of life on the high seas and on a deserted tropical island in the seventeenth or eighteenth century. There have been many films, TV programmes and theatrical adaptations of this exciting novel.

In this edition, the original novel, *Robinson Crusoe*, has been shortened and retold to make it easier to read. The key characters and the storyline are preserved but presented in a simpler way that hopefully keeps some of the author's style in the process. A glossary is provided at the end of this book to help with unfamiliar words and phrases.

We have also provided some notes for the reader at the beginning of the book, including a summary of the plot, a look at the main themes, a short biography of Daniel Defoe, the historical context in which the book was written and a list of characters.

We have tried to explain the key elements in the book and why it was important at its time of publication, but as you read Crusoe's story it is important to remember that it was written almost three hundred years ago, when many things were very different and most of the world was yet to be charted on a map. There are some things in the book that we think are very wrong but that were quite common and accepted during Defoe's lifetime. For example, Robinson Crusoe thinks it is all right to buy and sell people as slaves. Slavery is cruel and unjust but we need to be aware that some of the cruelty shown towards slaves and indigenous people was an unconscious cruelty based on beliefs held by much of British society during Defoe's lifetime.

We hope that you enjoy this intriguing adventure story and that you go on to read the original novel.

Warning: spoilers follow! Skip these introductory pages if you want the story to remain a surprise.

Summary

Robinson Crusoe is an Englishman from the town of York in the seventeenth century. He is the youngest son of a merchant. His father wants him to become a man of business like him but Crusoe wants to go to sea instead. His father asks him to wait for a year and Crusoe tries to obey him but eventually he gives in to temptation and sets out on a ship bound for London with a friend. A storm at sea nearly causes the death of Crusoe and his friend but he soon forgets all about this and sets out to sea again. This voyage is a financial success, and leaving some of his profits in the care of a friendly widow, he goes to sea once more. This voyage ends in disaster when the ship is seized by Moorish pirates and Crusoe becomes the slave of a powerful man in the north African town of Sallee. While on a fishing expedition for his "owner", Crusoe and a slave boy called Xury escape and sail down the African coast. A kindly Portuguese captain picks them up, buys the slave boy from Crusoe and takes Crusoe to Brazil. In Brazil, Crusoe establishes himself as a plantation owner and soon becomes successful. He is asked by friends to lead an expedition to Guinea to trade for slaves. He sets sail from Brazil bound for Guinea but ends up shipwrecked on a small island off the coast of Trinidad.

Crusoe soon learns he is the sole survivor of the

expedition apart from the ship's dog and two cats. Needing shelter and food, he returns to the beached remains of his ship twelve times to salvage guns, gunpowder, food, and other items. He builds himself a shelter surrounded by a stockade (see page 61) and a "cellar" in which to store anything that needs to be sheltered from the rain and the sun. He then sets out to explore the island. He finds some wild goats he can kill for meat. He keeps a journal of all his activities on the island. He falls ill and after recovering, he reads the Bible and becomes religious, thanking God for his fate in which nothing is missing but other human beings. Venturing further into the island, he finds a pleasant valley with lots of grape vines where he builds a shady shelter. He begins to feel more optimistic about being on the island, describing himself as its "king". He trains a pet parrot and develops skills in basket-weaving, breadmaking and pottery. He cuts down an enormous cedar tree and builds a huge canoe from its trunk, but he discovers that it is too large and he cannot move it to the sea. After building a smaller boat, he rows around the island but is swept away by a powerful current. He eventually makes it back to the shore where he hears his parrot calling his name and is thankful for being saved once again. He spends several years in peace.

One day, Crusoe is shocked to discover a man's footprint on the beach. He first assumes the footprint is the devil's, then decides it must belong to one of the cannibals (people who eat other humans) said to live in the region. Terrified, he arms himself and remains on the lookout for visiting cannibals. One day, he sees a boat sailing away from the island and he makes his way to the beach where he thinks the boat must have left from. He is horrified to discover that the beach is covered in human bones, apparently the remains of a cannibal feast. Alarmed, he continues to keep a lookout for more cannibals.

Some eighteen months later, Crusoe catches sight of thirty cannibals heading for shore with two victims. They kill one of the victims. The second one suddenly breaks free and runs along the beach towards Crusoe who protects him, defeating most of the cannibals in the process. The victim falls to his knees in front of Crusoe in gratitude. Crusoe names him Friday, to commemorate the day on which his life was saved. Crusoe decides Friday will make a good servant.

Friday is cheerful and willing to work hard whatever the task. Once Friday has learned some English, Crusoe teaches him about God and helps him to learn all the things he has had to learn as a castaway on the island. Friday informs Crusoe that there are some Spanish seamen living with his people on the mainland and Crusoe decides to make contact with these Spaniards. Just as they are about to set sail they are surprised by the arrival of more cannibals in canoes. One of the victims being held by the cannibals is in European dress. Friday and Crusoe kill most of the cannibals and release the European—a Spaniard. Friday is overjoyed to find his father lying tied up in the bottom of one of the canoes. The four men return to Crusoe's shelter for food and rest. All agree to try and fetch the Spaniards from the mainland so that they can help them build a boat that would be big enough to take them all to the American colonies. Friday's father and the Spaniard are sent off in advance to the mainland in one of the captured canoes.

Before they return, a large English ship appears near the island. Crusoe is suspicious. They watch as eleven men bring three prisoners onto the beach in a longboat. One of the prisoners is the captain of the ship, which has been taken in a mutiny. Friday and Crusoe rescue the captives and with their help they eventually overpower the mutineers. They persuade the captured mutineers to help retake the ship from the mutineers still on the ship.

When the ship has been seized, Crusoe and the captain suggest to a group of the mutineers that they would be better staying on the island than coming back to England where they would surely be hanged. Crusoe instructs them on all the skills they will need to survive on the island and tells them to expect the arrival of the Spaniards in due course. Then at last he and Friday board the English ship and sail for England. Crusoe had been away from England for thirty-five years and a castaway on his island for twenty-eight years.

Please note that in this edition of *Robinson Crusoe* the story ends here, missing out the final section of the original book which ends with one last adventure as Crusoe and Friday fight off famished wolves while crossing the Pyrenees.

Themes

Themes that are repeated or developed in *Robinson Crusoe* include religion, wealth, class and society, mastery and slavery, and the so-called "savages" (Defoe's term) who inhabit Crusoe's world.

Religion

The theme of religion is behind the very structure of the book, *Robinson Crusoe*. The story follows its hero Robinson Crusoe on a spiritual journey that begins with transgression (sin—his rebellion against his parents by going to sea despite their wish for him to go into trade); retribution (punishment—a series of successive shipwrecks that eventually land him on a deserted island); repentance (the painful lessons of life on a desert island); and finally redemption (Crusoe's conversion of himself and others to Christianity and his return to England). To begin with, whenever Crusoe is in a difficult situation he often tries to strike a bargain with God ("Spare my life and I promise never to set foot on a ship again") and he is quite cynical about God's response to a cry for help ("It seemed that God had turned a deaf ear to Jeremiah's prayer"). However, whenever he is in danger, he always asks for God's help, and as he recovers from a serious illness, he begins to read his Bible and asks God to forgive his sins. After this, he talks of his "Christian duty" and believes that "all help is from Heaven". He also shows an understanding and tolerance of other beliefs ("And it amused me that while I was a Protestant and had instructed Friday in that religion, his father was a pagan cannibal and the Spaniard a Catholic. As fair a mix of religions as would be found in kingdoms many times the size of mine").

Wealth

At the beginning of the book, Crusoe reveals that personal wealth is important to his family. His father has done very well for himself in business as a trader and he is anxious for his son to do the same. The young Crusoe says he isn't interested in a career in trade and runs away to sea to avoid having to work for his father. But he later becomes quite wealthy himself, making lots of money in Africa and in his sugar plantation in Brazil (thanks in large part to the slave trade that existed at that time).

However, when he is marooned on a desert island, he no longer has any material wealth and he comes to appreciate that happiness does not depend on having lots of money. When he finds thirty-six pounds in coins on the wreck of the ship that had left him stranded on a desert island he says, "What good are these to a man in my situation?" He takes pleasure from the fact that he can look after himself and enjoys all the practical tasks that make his life more secure and comfortable. When he has finished constructing his "bower" he is able to joke about his situation, comparing it to the lifestyle of wealthy people back in England ("I now had a seaside house and a country house").

Class and society

According to his father, Crusoe's family is a middle-class family. His father recognizes that some elements of society are too rich and some too poor but he considers that they are in the middle between the rich and the poor and happy as a result. He wants the same for his son but Crusoe chooses to abandon his family and its middle-class society for a life at sea. However, when he eventually finds himself on a desert island, he goes about creating a social order of his own and soon the island has a society which reflects to some extent the English society he abandoned in his youth.

To begin with, Crusoe only has his animal friends but eventually he is joined by Friday, the Spaniard, Friday's father and the mutineering Englishmen. Crusoe sees himself as the "king" of the island and later describes himself as its "governor". Friday (and Friday's father) are at the lower end of the island's social order. Crusoe feels superior to Friday and only ever sees him as a servant. Their master-servant relationship, as described by Defoe, is nevertheless much better than it would have been in real life at this time.

Cut off from the society that he was once so eager to leave behind, there are times on the island when it seems that Crusoe is quite happy to be on his own and at one with nature. He manages to make a life for himself despite his circumstances and a life that contains some pleasures—for example, his appreciation for the landscape where he sets up his "bower". When he finds the footprint, he is not immediately excited at the possibility of there being another Englishman on the island who might be able to help him get back to civilization. Instead he is frightened that the footprint belongs to "savages" who are likely to be a threat to his island existence (or even that the footprint belongs to the devil).

Mastery and slavery

Mastery means control or superiority over something or someone and in *Robinson Crusoe* we are talking about Crusoe's mastery over himself, his environment and some of the people he meets on his adventures. The young Crusoe first takes charge of his life after he abandons his parents and goes to sea against their wishes. Although he experiences great danger at sea he feels that he has the world at his feet and he goes on to make a great success of his first long voyage. When he is captured by pirates, he becomes a slave (a person legally owned by another and having no freedom of action or right to property) and, while he is able to cope with the demands of this new life, he never stops thinking about escape. As a slave he does not enjoy having no mastery over his own life. He becomes a successful "plantationer" after his escape from the pirates and is soon a wealthy man in control of his own future once again.(Although he has experienced what it feels like to be a slave, he is happy, for example, to agree to a trip to bring more slaves from Africa to work on his friend's plantations and his own.)

It is when he is shipwrecked and washed up on the

island that he really shows that he is the master of himself and his environment ("I was learning more and more, not just about the island but about myself"). He is able to create a home for himself and find food and fill his days in a calm and rational manner. He seems to be in complete control of himself and his life as a castaway.

Crusoe immediately assumes superiority over Xury and over Friday and, in keeping with the idealized notion of the time that a slave accepts and thinks of his master as his superior, they both seem to accept their positions as his slaves or "servants". (Defoe uses the word "servant" for slaves who serve Crusoe personally but they are not paid for their work.)

However, there is something a little more between Crusoe and Friday than a simple master and slave relationship—there is a kind of understanding between them that makes their relationship one of mutual respect. This would have been very unlikely in the wider society of the time, for in the eighteenth century when slavery was common, a slave was seldom thought of as an individual with all the attributes of any normal human being—a slave was a commodity to be bought and sold.

"Savages"

The word "savages" is used by Defoe to describe the native population of the lands close to Crusoe's island at a time when, out of ignorance, native or indigenous peoples were regarded by most people as primitive, uncivilized, brutal and fierce. This view of indigenous peoples gave Europeans of the time an excuse to establish colonies without considering the possibility of pre-existing, functional societies among the indigenous peoples. Nowadays this usage of the word would be regarded as archaic and offensive.

Crusoe describes Friday as handsome, intelligent, brave and loyal (not qualities usually associated with "savages" in Defoe's time). Perhaps Defoe had been exposed to the idea of the "noble savage"—an idea held by those who believed that "savages" who had not been "corrupted" by civilization symbolized the idea that humans are essentially good. In 1784, Benjamin Franklin, talking about native Americans, said "Savages we call them, because their manners differ from ours, which we think the perfection of civility; they think the same of theirs." But it is more likely that Crusoe considered Friday's attributes from the perspective of a "master" praising a loyal servant. In *Robinson Crusoe*, Crusoe represents the so-called "educated European" while Friday is a "savage" who can only be saved from his barbarous way of life by becoming part of Crusoe's culture and society.

The Life of Daniel Defoe

Daniel Defoe was an English trader who had done a lot of travelling as part of his job. He was also the author of more than five hundred books, journals and pamphlets on various topics. His novel *Robinson Crusoe* was one of the first English novels to be written and its simple narrative style has helped to make it one of the most widely published books in history.

No-one knows exactly when or where Daniel Defoe was born but most agree he was born Daniel Foe in or around 1660 in London. He was the son of James Foe, a London butcher and tallow chandler (a person who makes or sells candles of tallow, a hard fat taken from dead animals). His mother, Annie, died when he was about ten. He later changed his surname to the more aristocratic name of Defoe.

His parents were Dissenters—Christians who separated from the Church of England and established their own churches, schools and communities. Some Dissenters emigrated to the "New World" (the Americas). Defoe first attended a boarding school in Dorking and then studied at a Dissenters' academy in London. In his youth, Daniel lived through the Great Plague, the Great Fire of London, a series of Dutch attacks on London and the persecution of Dissenters.

He went into business as a young man and had a reasonably successful career as a general merchant, buying and selling a variety of goods from wine to woollen goods and making enough money at one stage to buy a country estate. As a general merchant, he would have travelled abroad and been familiar with ships and life at sea.

He also acted as a secret agent for William III and for a while he was responsible for the collection of a tax on glass imposed by the British government of the time. However, he was often in debt and by 1703 he had given up being a merchant for good.

During his lifetime, Defoe was a very versatile writer. He wrote many books and produced a lot of political and religious pamphlets as well as many journals on various topics. He was charged with libel over one religious pamphlet and part of his punishment was to stand in a pillory at the mercy of the mob (1703). A pillory was a wooden framework into which offenders were locked by the neck and wrists. Passing members of the public could hurl abuse at the offender as well as missiles ranging from rotten fruit and vegetables to mud, excrement, dead rats, and even stones.

Defoe worked as a political agent (an official diplomatic position) and he was a spy for Robert Harley, Chancellor of the Exchequer, in the year leading up to the Anglo-Scottish Union of 1707. In 1713, his political opponents had him imprisoned for his writing in the *Review*, a periodical that was published from 1704 to 1713. In 1719, Defoe wrote his first novel, *Robinson Crusoe*, and few more novels followed until his last major fiction piece *Roxana* in 1724. In the last few years of his life he continued to write on a wide variety of topics. He died in 1731.

Defoe's Life in *Robinson Crusoe*

Consciously or unconsciously many authors borrow experiences from their own lives when writing their books.

Defoe reveals a lot of his own personal background in Robinson Crusoe. He was a general merchant—buying and selling a variety of goods—for many years before he took up writing full time so he understood the ups and downs of life for someone involved in trading. Crusoe's father is a trader and he has done well for himself.

Defoe's financial successes and failures (he went bankrupt at least twice) are also reflected in Crusoe's life as Crusoe, like Defoe, experiences the financial ups and downs that life can throw at you (often through no fault of your own) from going to sea for the first time without a penny to his name to enjoying great wealth as a plantation owner. Defoe travelled a lot and would have undoubtedly spent time on ships and been familiar with the perils of being at sea. His vivid descriptions of ships caught up in storms in *Robinson Crusoe* almost certainly come from his personal experience of such storms during his travels.

Defoe acted as a secret agent/spy for King William III and some of Crusoe's behaviour in certain situations is the sort of thing you would expect from a spy who was good at his job. Both his resourcefulness (when he plans his escape from his life as a slave, for example) and his inventiveness (when he lands on a deserted island and sets about creating a safe and relatively comfortable existence for himself without any help) reflect his ability to do what he needs to do to survive, whatever the circumstances.

In his many writings, Defoe often explores religious issues and it is obvious that Christianity played as important a part in his life as it does in Crusoe's. Although a lot is written in the Bible about how to treat slaves, it is a little strange to the modern reader that Defoe and his main character, Crusoe, as committed Christians, were quite accepting of slavery and what they saw as their natural superiority over servants, slaves and "savages". We need to be aware that Defoe was reflecting how people saw slavery in his day and you should keep this in mind when reading *Robinson Crusoe*.

Historical Context

The seventeenth century (in which *Robinson Crusoe* is set) was a century of bloody civil war, revolution and religious persecution in Great Britain. It was also the time of the Great Plague of London (1665) and the Great Fire of London (1666). Many people set sail from Britain to find a new life in the colonies. In 1620, the "Pilgrim Fathers", for example, left England to escape religious persecution and landed on the coast of what is now Massachusetts in America.

As the population of the New World colonies grew, landowners wanted help to develop their land. This demand for labour resulted in a race-based transatlantic slave trade, when black slaves were shipped from Africa across the Atlantic Ocean to the new colonies. By 1699, about eighty per cent of the people living in the Caribbean were slaves and slavery had become central to the economy of the new colonies. Slavery in the seventeenth century was a legally recognized system in which humans were treated as property. They could be bought and sold (sometimes for profit, sometimes as slave labour) by their "masters". A person working as a slave was usually treated badly and had no personal rights.

Crusoe's story reveals some of the attitudes and behaviour of society at a time when transatlantic slavery was an accepted fact of life. References to slavery have been left in this edition of Robinson Crusoe in keeping with the original text. Slavery was finally abolished in the British Empire with the Slavery Abolition Act of 1833 and in the U. S. with the 13th amendment to the U. S. Constitution in 1865. Although slavery is no longer legal anywhere in the world, human trafficking remains an international scandal and more than twenty million people are living in illegal slavery today.

In the eighteenth century, Britain held a dominant position among the European trading countries. Most of this trade was very reliant on ships carrying goods by sea around the world. British ships, for example, became the largest and most efficient carriers of slaves from Africa to the new colonies.

There were many stories of real castaways in Defoe's time that could have been Defoe's inspiration for his main character Robinson Crusoe. The best known of these was Alexander Selkirk (1676–1721), a Scottish sailor who spent more than four years as a castaway after being marooned on an uninhabited island in the South Pacific Ocean. Another was ship's surgeon

Henry Pitman whose story (published in 1689) of being shipwrecked and stuck on a desert island may also have been the inspiration for *Robinson Crusoe*.

Significant events in the UK in 1719

(when *Robinson Crusoe* was first published)

- Westminster Hospital in London is founded
- Thomas Fleet publishes *Mother Goose's Melodies For Children*
- British Government forces defeat an alliance of Jacobite and Spanish forces at the Battle of Glen Shiel in Scotland
- An attempted invasion of Britain by Spain fails
- Brook Taylor publishes *New Principles of Linear Perspective* (a form of perspective in which parallel lines are represented as converging so as to give the illusion of depth and distance)
- In London, a measles epidemic and a smallpox epidemic are followed by a severe influenza epidemic
- Joseph Addison, English poet, writer and politician, dies aged 47
- (John) Lombe's Silk Mill is the first successful silk throwing mill in England and probably the first fully mechanized factory in the world
- The first recorded display of the aurora borealis ("the Northern Lights") in north American colonies

The Narrative

This book is written like an autobiography, so much so that when it was first published many people thought that Robinson Crusoe was a real person and the book was a description of his life on a real desert island. It is a first-person narrative which means it is written from the point of view of one person (the main character of the book, Robinson Crusoe). It is also written in the past tense.

"Narrative" is another word for a story or a written account of something. In a first-person narrative you will read: "**I** looked out to sea" and "**they** ran way". The narrative voice of Crusoe is calm, unhurried and conversational but it can convey fear and excitement. Crusoe tells us what he is doing in great detail and in such a personal way that we can't help getting caught up in his adventures. However the narrative can be seen as unreliable because we only get his point of view. For example, there is no-one who can challenge Crusoe's ideas about slavery—we have to assume that in his day everyone thought this way about slavery and this may not have been the case.

Robinson Crusoe was one of the first novels to be labelled as "realistic fiction". This is due in part to the fact that Crusoe tells his own story in a detached and rational manner. As the narrator he gives detailed descriptions of facts and objects. He measures and counts everything, uses specific dates and real places and he keeps a daily journal.

The Main Characters

Robinson Crusoe

Robinson Crusoe is the novel's protagonist (main character) and narrator. As a young middle-class man in York, England, Crusoe yearns for a life at sea but his father wants him to become a merchant like him. Crusoe rebels and sets sail on the first of many voyages. He is resourceful and practical in most situations and he survives storms, enslavement and twenty-eight years on a desert island.

The captain's widow

She is the wife of the first captain to take the young Crusoe under his wing. When the captain dies after taking Crusoe on a successful trading voyage to Guinea in Africa, Crusoe chooses to leave his savings with the captain's widow while he sets off on another voyage to Guinea. She looks after his money with great care. Her character, like Friday's, reminds us of the goodwill and trustworthiness of humans.

The Portuguese captain

The Portuguese captain picks up Crusoe and the slave boy Xury from their boat after they escape from their Moorish captors and float down the African coast. He is a good, honest man who plays an almost fatherly role in Crusoe's life by helping him to become a successful plantationer (the owner or manager of a plantation).

Friday

Friday belongs to a group of cannibals who live on the mainland (referred to as "savages" by Crusoe). He is rescued from certain death by Crusoe and he willingly becomes Crusoe's servant. Friday is the first person Crusoe introduces into the social order of the island. He is a servant and therefore Crusoe's inferior, but Friday is handsome, intelligent, brave and loyal.

The Spaniard

The Spaniard is one of the prisoners saved by Crusoe when cannibals bring him to the island with the intention of eating him. In exchange, he becomes a new "subject" in Crusoe's "kingdom" and is happy to fall in with Crusoe's plans to make a boat large enough to carry them all, including his fellow sailors living with the cannibals, to the colonies in America.

The English captain

The crew of the English captain have mutinied and he is rescued by Crusoe. He is more than ready to fight to get his ship back but he shows some compassion towards the mutineers (who face the death penalty for their crime) when he tells Crusoe he doesn't want to kill all of them—only the two ringleaders. He too becomes part of the island's social order when he refers to Crusoe as the "governor" of the island. He is happy to take Crusoe and Friday back to England.

List of Characters

ROBINSON CRUSOE, the novel's main character

MR. AND MRS. CRUSOE, Crusoe's parents

TOM BENTLEY, an old school friend of Crusoe

JEREMIAH, a boatswain

CAPTAIN BENTLEY, Tom's father

CAPTAIN — , the captain of the ship on which Crusoe makes his first voyage to Guinea

CAPTAIN — 'S WIDOW, whom Crusoe entrusts with his money

CAPTAIN OF THE MOROCCAN PIRATES, he captures and enslaves Crusoe

XURY (pronounced zoo-ree), a young Maresco boy of Islamic, Spanish and northwest African heritage

ISMAEL, second in command to the Moroccan pirate captain

PORTUGUESE CAPTAIN, he rescues Crusoe and Xury and teaches Crusoe how to be a plantationer

FRIDAY, the cannibal who becomes Crusoe's servant

SPANISH CAPTAIN, he is rescued from the cannibals by Crusoe

FRIDAY'S FATHER, also rescued from the same cannibals by Crusoe

ENGLISH CAPTAIN, he and his mate and a passenger are rescued from his mutineering crew by Crusoe and Friday

MUTINEERS, the crew of the English captain's ship who have mutinied and taken control of the ship

Robinson Crusoe

Chapter One

I Go to Sea

I was born in York in 1632, of a good family, although not of that country. My father was a Dutch merchant who had settled in England and done very well for himself in trade, first at Hull and afterwards at York, where he had married my mother.

Before her marriage to my father, my mother had been a Miss Robinson, and it was after her that I was named Robinson Kreutznaer.

The good people of York, finding it difficult to get their tongues around Kreutznaer, called our family Crusoe, and so I became known as Robinson Crusoe.

I was the third son of the family. My eldest brother, a soldier, was killed fighting the Spanish, and I have no idea what happened to my other brother.

Although my father's business was doing well, it was not, I thought, doing well enough to support me, so I decided to go to sea.

"You shall not!" my father stormed when I told him of my plans.

"But there is nothing for me here," I said.

"How can you say that?" my father went on. "You could go into trade, as I did. And look how well I've done."

"But I have no head for business," I protested.

"Robinson," said my father, sounding as if he was pleading with me. "Wait for a year. I'll do whatever I can to help you, to teach you the ways of business. And if after that you still wish to go to sea, ask me again."

I was almost eighteen. A whole year seemed like an eternity to me, but I agreed to what my father had said, and during the months that followed I tried to concentrate on what he would have me do.

But it was no good. Somehow, I had been born with salt in my veins and the call of the sea would not be denied.

When the year was up, I went to my father, but despite his promise, he refused to yield. A wise and grave man, he told me that a life at sea was for men of desperate fortune on the one hand or of superior fortune on the other. I belonged to the middle state, neither poor nor rich, and in his experience the best state in the world.

In despair, I decided to ask my mother to intervene.

"Mother," I said, "I still want to go to sea. Please can you help me persuade father."

"Robinson," she said, "you know very well what your father thinks of that."

"Please, mother," I pleaded. "Persuade him to let me go for a year. If, after that time, I decide the sea is not for me, after all, I will come home and work harder than he does at his business. I promise."

Mother looked at me for a moment.

"Robinson," she said, "I will tell your father what

you have just promised, but I will not try to persuade him one way or the other."

My father still refused to yield.

A few weeks after I had spoken to my mother, just after my nineteenth birthday, I decided to go to Hull for a few days. There was no reason for my decision—it was, as my mother would have said, a whim.

As I sat by the harbour watching ship after ship take to sea on the tide, how I wished I could have been on one of them.

I saw myself standing on deck, feeling the wind on my face as my ship approached a foreign port.

"Robinson Crusoe!" A voice stirred me from my daydream. "What are you doing in Hull?"

I looked round and saw my old school friend, Tom Bentley, standing before me.

"Tom!" I cried, slapping him on the shoulder. "How are you?"

"All the better for seeing you," he replied.

"We must find somewhere to go and celebrate our meeting," I said. "Come, there's an inn over there."

"I can't," said Tom. "My father's ship is about to sail for London, and I must be on it."

"Your father's ship?" I cried.

Tom nodded. "Why not join me?" he said. "You look as if you have little else to do, and it will cost you nothing."

And so, on the first day of September, 1651, without telling my mother or my father what I was about to do, I went to sea.

33

Chapter Two

Sailing into a Storm

It wasn't long before I wished I had stayed on dry land. A few hours out of port, the wind began to blow and the sea rose in a frightful manner.

"Are you all right, Robinson?" Tom shouted to make himself heard above the howling wind.

"I think I'm going to be sick," I moaned and dashed to the bows before I threw up over the deck.

"It's a judgement from Heaven," I sobbed as wave after wave of nausea washed over me. "I should never have disobeyed my parents."

The weather worsened, tossing the boat around like a feather caught in the wind.

"Please, God," I prayed, "spare my life and I promise never to set foot on a ship again. I'll go home to York and work hard at business and make my father proud of me."

By the time night fell, the gale had abated and the waves had fallen. I slept soundly, and when I woke up the next morning, it was a beautiful day.

The wind had fallen to a light breeze and the sea was as calm as a millpond.

My fears of the day before were soon forgotten as we sailed southwards.

I stood on deck watching the coastal villages we

passed come into view then fade in the distance, and I felt the world was at my feet.

I got to know the crew, and when one of them offered me a tot of rum I gladly accepted. It wasn't long before we were joined by another, then another, and soon we were all drinking more than was good for us and I was singing sea shanties as lustily as the next man.

We sailed on until we were off Yarmouth, where the breeze dropped completely and we found ourselves becalmed.

"Don't worry," said Tom, "we'll soon be on our way."

He was wrong. For eight days we lay off Yarmouth.

Just when I thought we were going to stay there forever, the wind began to blow and we headed south again. But a few hours later, it had risen to a gale and we sailed into a storm that made the one I had experienced on my first day at sea the merest squall.

For days the wind howled.

For days we were at the mercy of waves that towered above us, tossing us this way and that.

Great flashes of lightning cracked in the sky.

Driving rain made it impossible to stay on deck for more than a few minutes.

This time I was not the only one who was afraid.

Even Tom looked terrified, and when the mate said that he had never known a storm like it, the rest of the crew nodded in agreement.

We were huddled in the crew's quarters below deck.

"I wonder how long this is going to last for?" said the boatswain, a gloomy-looking man named Jeremiah. No sooner had he spoken than there was a loud splintering sound and water started to gush through a hole that appeared in the ship's timbers at his back.

"Man the pumps!" someone cried.

A few seconds later I was pumping as if my life depended on it, which, on reflection, it did.

It seemed that the more we pumped the more the water gushed through the leak.

"Harder, lads, harder!" the captain shouted, but when it became obvious that we were fighting a losing battle, he fought his way to his cabin and came back carrying an armful of distress flares.

Somehow he managed to light a taper and fired one of them into the air, followed by another, then another.

"Please, God," wailed Jeremiah, "let someone see them."

It seemed that God had turned a deaf ear to Jeremiah's prayer and that we were all about to go to a watery grave when someone shouted, "Look! A ship!"

We watched as a lightship heaved into view.

"The sea is far too heavy for them to launch a boat to save us."

I think that Jeremiah, who had just spoken, didn't want to be saved.

But they did it. Somehow the men in the lightship launched one of their boats, and when it was alongside our stricken ship, we managed to clamber aboard.

Later, when we were taken ashore, we found Tom's father waiting for us.

"I think," he said to me after he had heard our story,

"that you should take this as a warning and never go to sea again. If you do, you will meet with nothing but disasters and disappointments."

"Here," he went on, handing me some guineas, "take these and go back to York."

Chapter Three

A Capture and an Escape

For a while I was tempted to do as Tom's father had said, return to York. But the thought of what my father would say, and the way my friends would no doubt sneer at me, quickly drove that idea from my head—at least for the time being—and I set off for London.

A few days after I arrived in the city, I happened to meet some jolly fellows with whom I quickly made friends. One of them, a ship's captain, told me that he was about to sail for Guinea, on the coast of Africa, to trade with the people there.

"Join us," he said.

Memories of the storm off Yarmouth flooded through my mind.

"You can travel free," he went on.

I remembered Tom's father's warning.

"There's good money to be made."

We sailed a few days later.

With a calm sea and a fresh following wind, we reached Africa in good time.

At our first port of call, on the advice of my new friend, the captain, I spent some of my money on baubles and trinkets.

And when we anchored at harbours farther along the coast, I was able to trade my purchases for better things, and later I was able to use these to barter for gold dust.

By the time we sailed for home, I had five pounds nine ounces of the precious element in my bags, and when I returned to London I sold it for three hundred pounds! My father would have been proud of me!

Sadly, not long after we docked, the captain caught the fever and died.

"What now, Robinson?" his widow asked me when I called to pay my respects. "Home to York?"

I shook my head. "No!" I said, "I'm going back to Guinea."

"What!" she cried. "You're going to risk all your profit in another venture?"

"Not all," I said, "just one hundred pounds! Will you keep my other two hundred for me?"

"Of course," she said.

A week or two later, I was back at sea. Once again the weather was fine and we made good progress heading for the Canary Islands.

"Ship ahoy!" cried the watch one day when we were sailing off a port called Sallee, in the Emperor of Morocco's domain.

"That's no ordinary trader," cried one of the men. "That's a pirate ship."

As quickly as we could, we raised all the sails, hoping to outrun the fast-approaching vessel, but it had the advantage of the wind and bore down on us.

Soon, she was so close that we could see the faces of her crew quite clearly.

"Turks!" There was fear in the skipper's voice.

No sooner had he spoken than a cannon was fired across our bows.

We rolled our few guns into position, trying to catch them broadside, but they were too quick for us.

It was soon plainly obvious that the pirates were better equipped than we were. As they came alongside, we were unable to stop them swarming aboard.

We fought bravely, but we were outnumbered and easily beaten. With pirates at the helm, our brave little ship was taken to Sallee.

"You," their captain said in remarkably good English, tugging my long hair so hard that I thought it would be torn out, "what's your name?"

"Robinson Crusoe," I said through gritted teeth.

"You're no ordinary sailor," he went on.

"I'm a merchant!" I said.

"Not any longer," spat my captor. "You're my slave."

And so, miserable slave that I now was, I was taken to his house overlooking the shore.

My new master put me to work around the house—cleaning, sweeping and doing other things that I had always had done for me.

My life was not as bad as it could have been. Although I no longer had my liberty, my new master was not cruel and treated me well, but even so there was not one minute that passed when I did not dream of my freedom.

One morning, after I had been in Sallee for a few weeks, my master called for me.

"We're going fishing," he said.

"Just the two of us?" I asked.

"No! We'll take that young Maresco boy with us."

I had fished before, when I was a child—what lad hasn't sat by a stream hoping that a passing trout will take the bait, hooked onto the end of a piece of string? But this was different.

We scudded across the water in the small boat my master used for fishing until, after about half an hour at sea, he told me and the Maresco lad, whose name was Xury, to drop our lines into the water.

When we hauled them in, there was a fish on every hook, and soon the bottom of the boat was so full of wriggling, writhing fish that it looked as if a stream of silver was flowing down the middle of the boat.

We went fishing quite often after that day, my master, the Maresco boy and I, and I soon became better than my master at knowing where to drop the lines to get the best catch.

One day, when I had been in my master's service for several months, we were out fishing when from out of nowhere a fog descended—a fog so dense that I could hardly see my master who was sitting at the other end of the boat.

For hour after hour we drifted in the thick fog, and by the time it had lifted we were much farther out to sea than we had been, and it took us another two hours to reach our harbour.

"Next time we go out," said my master, "we're taking food and water with us in case we are fogbound again."

"And," he went on, "firearms. Who knows what sort of sea monster may surprise us. And if a passing fowl comes into range, then all the better, for we can shoot her for the pot."

Chapter Four

Escape from Slavery

"Robinson," said my master one morning when I was hoeing weeds in the garden. "I'm having guests for dinner tonight and I would like to serve them fish."

"Are we to take the boat out, master?" I asked.

"You are," he said, "and Xury. I'm too busy."

The thought of escape, never far from my mind, reared up again, and the expression on my face must have changed, for my master went on, "And just in case you have any thought of trying to get away, my second in command, Ismael, will be with you."

I knew the Moor well, and from what I had overheard during his conversations with my master, I knew him to be a cruel, mean man.

I called for Xury, and the two of us made our way to the harbour where Ismael was waiting impatiently for us.

"You," he said to Xury, "take the tiller. And you," he went on, pointing at me, "untie the rope."

"Have you brought provisions?" I asked, innocently.

"There's plenty on board," he growled.

"But those are my master's," I said. "Surely you would not presume to use the master's food and water?"

"You're right," he said, after a moment.

By the time we sailed, we had taken on fresh

43

provisions, not just food and water, for I had also taken the opportunity to smuggle some beeswax, thread and twine, an axe, a saw and a hammer on board, and I had made sure we were well stocked with powder and shot for the fowling pistols.

We sailed until we came to a spot not far from the coast where I knew there would be no fish. Nonetheless, I feigned surprise when I drew in my lines and saw there was nothing on them.

"We need to go further out," I said, "to where the water is deeper."

The sun was high in the sky when I threw my lines over again. Immediately I had done that, I bent down as if to pick something off the deck behind the spot where Ismael was standing. As I stood up, I gave him a mighty shove and, taken by surprise, he lost his balance and fell into the water with a loud splash.

"Fool," he spluttered, swimming towards the boat. "Here, give me a hand to get in."

By this time I had a fowling piece in my hand. "Lay one hand on this boat and I'll shoot," I called, aiming the gun at him.

"I'll have you flogged to within an inch of your life for this," Ismael shouted. "Now help me aboard."

"You're an excellent swimmer," I laughed. "It shouldn't take you too long to reach the shore.

I turned to Xury, who was standing staring at me in open-mouthed astonishment.

"Are you with me?" I asked.

He nodded.

"And will you swear to be loyal to me?"

Again he nodded.

"Good lad."

I knew that Ismael would be watching to see which direction I would take, and I was well aware that he would expect me to sail north towards the Straits of Gibraltar. No-one in his right mind would sail southward to the lands of the Barbarians, men who would paddle out to our boat in their canoes as soon as they saw us and take us back to be cooked in their pots.

But, intending to fool the Moor, I sailed north until dusk, and then turned and sailed south, then east.

On and on we sailed, putting hundreds of miles between us and the Emperor of Morocco's lands, and after five days we dropped anchor in the mouth of a little river.

Xury and I decided to stay in the boat until nightfall and then swim ashore when it was dark to try to find fresh water, but when darkness came, we heard so many animals roar and growl that we thought it wiser to stay in the boat.

When daylight came, setting aside our fear of being taken captive by savages, we took the boat in as close to the shore as she would go and then waded to the beach, carrying two water jars with us.

I was wary of going too far from the boat, but Xury had no such apprehensions. I watched as he made his way into the scrubland until he had disappeared from sight.

Suddenly, I heard a gunshot and a few moment later Xury came running towards me.

I fully expected him to be pursued by natives, but when he came close I saw he had a large hare-like animal hanging round his shoulders.

"Look what I shot," he said proudly.

"Did you find fresh water?" I asked and was greatly relieved when he nodded. I was even more relieved when he told me he had seen no wild men.

I had no navigational instruments to help me work out precisely where I was, but I assumed that we were in the barren, uninhabited lands that lie between the Emperor of Morocco's dominions and the Africans' lands far to the south.

We took on as much fresh water as we had room for, returned to our boat and sailed on down the coast, seeing nothing but dull, arid lands.

Once or twice I thought I saw the mountains of Tenerife in the distance, but the winds and heavy seas prevented us from heading for them, and we sailed on, hugging the coast, landing when we needed to take on fresh water.

On and on we sailed, hoping to reach the Cape Verde Islands before our supplies ran out, for I knew that ships from Europe stopped there on their way to and from Guinea, the East Indies and Brazil.

One day, when we had been at sea for more than ten days, I was in the cabin when I heard Xury shout, "Master, a ship with a sail!"

I rushed to the helm and saw a Portuguese caravel

shortening her sail to let our little vessel catch up with her.

When I explained to the captain that I had just escaped from the Moors, he took Xury and me and our meagre possessions aboard.

Chapter Five

I Become a Planter

"Where are you bound for, sir?" I asked the captain later.

"Brazil," he replied.

I offered to pay for my passage, but he refused, saying that if he took what little I had I would surely starve in Brazil, and there was little use in sending to starvation a life he had just saved.

Even more generously, he offered to buy my boat, and when I said I would leave the price to him, he said he would give me eighty pieces of eight for it when we reached Brazil.

He also wanted to buy Xury!

"He has been very loyal to me," I said.

"How would it be if I purchase him from you and promise to give him his freedom in ten years' time if he becomes a Christian?"

Xury agreed, so the captain and I shook hands on the bargain, settling on a price of sixty pieces of eight.

When we reached port, on the first of November, the captain purchased all the equipment I had taken aboard at Sallee for another 220 pieces of eight, so when I stepped ashore, I had more than enough money to keep me going.

When I told my friend, the captain, about the 200

pounds I had in England, he advised me to send for half of it. "That way," he said, "if things go badly for you in Brazil, you will still have something should you return to London."

We agreed that when he reached Europe, he would take with him a letter to the widow who had my money, asking that she send one half of it to me.

My fortune seemed to be on the up, for I was recommended to lodge with a plantation owner who quickly became my friend.

From him I learned the planter's skills and, seeing how such men prospered, I decided I would become one myself.

I purchased as much land as my money allowed me to and set to work.

My plantation was in such a remote part of the country, so far from my nearest neighbour, that I sometimes thought that I lived just like a man cast away on a desert island that had no-one on it but himself.

For two years I managed to grow just enough fruit and vegetables for my own needs and little else. But by the third year I had cleared enough land to grow some sugar and tobacco, which I sold for a good profit.

I lost count of the number of times I regretted selling Xury, for an extra pair of hands would have been very useful.

By now my friend, the captain, had returned, bringing with him a servant for me whom he had bought with five pounds the widow had given him, so relieved was she that I was safe.

The captain had invested most of the hundred pounds I had sent for in a cargo that I was able to sell for a fine profit, more than enough to buy another slave and pay the wages of a servant.

The next year was an excellent one. I had a bumper crop of tobacco and I expanded my business substantially and increased my wealth a great deal.

It occurred to me one day that I had arrived at what my father would have called "the middle station in life", a position I would probably have attained if I had stayed in York and worked as hard as I had in Brazil, and would have done so without my life having been at risk as often as it had.

By now I had been in Brazil for four years. I spoke the language and had made friends, not just with fellow plantation owners but with merchants in San Salvadore, my nearest port.

I often dined with them and told them of my two trips to Guinea.

"Is it as easy to trade as you say?" asked one of my friends one night.

I nodded. "You buy trinkets in coastal towns—beads, toys, knives and the like—and when you get to remote parts, the natives are happy to trade what you have for gold dust, ivory and," I lowered my voice, "enemies from other tribes they have captured, which can be sold as slaves."

The next morning three of my acquaintances rode out to see me. "We have a proposition for you," one of them said.

"And what would that be?" I asked.

"We want to charter a ship to sail to Guinea and as you have been there we'd like you to lead the expedition."

"To trade for gold?" I said.

My friend shook his head. "No," he said. "Slaves!"

"A dangerous business," I said. "The kings of Spain and Portugal control the trade in slaves between Africa and South America. You'd never be able to sell them here without them finding out."

"We don't intend selling them," my friend went on, "we'll put them to work on our plantations."

"And what's in it for me?" I asked.

"One quarter of the men you bring back."

Now slaves in Brazil were scarce and expensive, and I was sorely tempted. "One condition," I said.

"What's that?"

"That you look after my plantation in my absence. Agreed?"

"Agreed!"

And so, on the first of September 1659, eight years to the day after I had set out from Hull, I set sail from Brazil bound for Guinea.

* * *

There were seventeen of us on board the 120-ton ship— me, the captain and his boy, and a crew of fourteen. The sun beat down from a cloudless sky, making it exceedingly hot as we sailed northwards along the coast of Brazil.

The fine weather continued all the way to the Equator, which we crossed after twelve days at sea. But no sooner were we in northern waters, than the weather worsened. The wind rose violently and swung round from the southeast to the northwest, and then settled into the northeast and stayed there for twelve days.

We were at the mercy of the sea, and I became convinced that we would not survive the storm. Sadly, one of the men and the cabin boy did not. The man died of fever and the poor lad was washed overboard by an enormous wave.

By the time the hurricane passed, our ship was leaking and was so battered that the captain wanted to head for port to make repairs.

However, on studying the charts, we calculated that there was no inhabited part of the mainland within easy sailing distance, so we decided to head for Barbados in the Caribbean.

But once again the weather worsened, and we found ourselves being blown farther and farther westwards.

It was early in the morning that one of the crew shouted, "Land ahoy!"

We rushed on deck, with no way of knowing if the land we were looking at was an island or part of the mainland, whether it was inhabited or deserted, fertile or barren.

Suddenly there was a mighty shudder and with a dreadful grating sound the ship ran aground. Towering waves crashed into her, and it seemed that it would be only a matter of time before she broke into pieces.

Death was staring us in the face.

Somehow the mate and some of the men slung the lifeboat over the side and we clambered into it. We managed to row towards the land, but as we neared it, a mountain of water slammed into our boat and we were swept into the water.

Down and down I plunged, feeling the enormous weight of the water crushing my lungs, but just as I thought they were about to burst, the water cleared and I gulped in lungful after lungful of air.

But again the sea came pouring over me, dashing me against sharp rocks that felt as if they were ripping my flesh from my bones.

Just as I thought I was about to die, I felt my feet touch the bottom. Summoning every ounce of my strength, I managed to stand up and found myself shoulder high in swirling water.

I filled my lungs with air again, just as another wave crashed into my back.

A few moments later, I found myself lying in the shallow waters of a sandy beach.

I was cut by the rocks.

My body felt as if it had been trampled on by galloping horses.

But I was alive.

Chapter Six

Castaway

I lay there, thanking God that I had been saved, and then got to my feet and walked along the beach. It was then that the true horror of my situation hit me—I had been saved, but the rest of my companions must have drowned, for the only sign I saw of them afterwards were three caps and two shoes.

I looked out to sea and saw the stricken ship almost submerged by the huge waves crashing into her. "Lord," I said to myself, "how was it possible that I got ashore?"

My situation seemed hopeless. Not only was I soaked through, with no dry clothes to change into, but I had nothing to eat or drink. For all I knew, even as I looked around me, wild animals, or worse, savages, may already be creeping up on me and I had nothing to defend myself with. All I had in my pockets were a small knife, a pipe and a battered old bag of tobacco.

Night was falling by now and I had to find somewhere safe to sleep. Looking around, I decided to spend the night in a thick bushy tree nearby, but first I was so thirsty I had to try to find something to drink.

Imagine my joy when, 200 yards along the beach, I found a creek with fresh water. I drank as much as I could hold then chewed some tobacco to keep hunger at bay. On my way back to the tree, I cut myself a branch to use as a club should I be attacked in the night, and then I clambered into my makeshift sleeping quarters.

I didn't expect to sleep, but I was so tired that the next thing I knew it was morning.

When I looked out to sea, I saw that the tide had moved the ship and that it looked as if she had been swept up onto the shore about two miles away.

I walked along the beach towards her until my way was blocked by an inlet about half a mile wide. I returned to my tree to puzzle out a way to get to her.

Just after noon, when the tide was out, I walked back to the inlet and found that I could wade to within 400 yards of the ship, close enough to see that she was still intact and that had we stayed on board we would have been safe. The thought that my companions had drowned needlessly brought tears to my eyes.

The intense heat had dried my clothes by now, so I took them off and swam to the ship, but when I got to her I found she was standing so high out of the water, that there was no way for me to climb aboard.

But as I swam around her, I spotted a piece of rope dangling over the side and, using every ounce of my strength, managed to climb up to the forecastle.

Once aboard I saw that although she had taken in a great deal of water, parts of the ship were dry and most of the ship's provisions were undamaged.

I filled my mouth with ship's biscuit and crammed as much as they would hold into my pockets. I swigged some rum, and for the first time since I had been swept into the sea I began to feel a little hope.

The ship was well stocked, but if another storm blew up, or a high tide rose, she could well be swept back out to sea, so I knew I had to get as many provisions to the shore as I could, and to do that I had to build myself a raft. I found some wood and some spare masts and, after tying rope to each one so they wouldn't float away, threw them overboard. Next, I splashed into the water and pulled them towards me. Four of the pieces I lashed together at both ends, then tied three or four shorter pieces crosswise on top of them.

I climbed onto my raft and quickly realized that although it would take my weight, it was not strong enough to carry much else. I struggled back onto the ship and set to work with the carpenter's saw and a spare top mast which I cut into three.

When I tied them to my raft, I was delighted to find it was now strong enough to carry me and a fair amount of provisions.

I loaded cheese, bread, rice, dried goat's meat, some rice and corn (which we had taken aboard to feed chickens that we had long since devoured) into seamen's chests, which I had emptied of their provisions, and loaded them onto my raft.

I found some liquor, and while I was stowing this alongside the chests, I was horrified to see that the clothes I had so carefully left on the beach were floating out to sea. All I had were the breeches and stockings I stood up in.

I rummaged for clothes in the crew's quarters and took enough for my immediate needs.

Next I found the carpenter's chest, more precious to me than a shipload of gold, two fowling pieces, two pistols, powder, shot, two rusty swords and an old oar.

My raft was now fairly well loaded. But just as I was about to leave I heard two pathetic "Miaows!"

Looking around, I saw the two ship's cats, whom I picked up and took aboard the raft.

Just as I clambered on, I heard something splash into the water. A few moments later, the ship's dog appeared, bobbing beside the raft.

Letting the incoming tide wash me to the shore, I was carried into a creek and, using a piece of mast as an oar, managed to steer into a little cove, close enough to the open sea for me to spot a passing ship but sheltered enough to provide some cover.

My raft and cargo safely ashore, I set out to explore the country, the dog at my ankles, and to find a proper place to build some sort of shelter. From then on, the dog was my faithful friend until the day he died many years later. The ship's cats I did not see again for many months, for as soon as we were on dry land they disappeared into the undergrowth and vanished.

As I looked around, I saw a hill about a mile away and, arming myself with a fowling piece and a pistol, I set off for it.

I was exhausted by the time I reached it, but I forced myself to climb up it and to look around.

I had hoped that I was on some continent. Imagine

my horror when I saw that I was on an island. Two smaller islands lay some way off and beyond them a vast expanse of sea.

I saw no sign of human habitation.

It seemed to me that I was alone—quite alone—with no other human close by for who knows how many miles.

I went back to the raft and started to unload it, which took me the rest of the day.

When night came, I barricaded myself in with the chests and the boards from my raft, making them into a kind of hut.

As I lay there, wondering how I could survive, I decided to return to the ship as soon as possible in the morning, for the next storm that blew may break her up completely.

I also made up my mind not to rebuild the raft, but to swim out to the ship as before and make a new one when I got there.

This time I took from the ship bags of nails and spikes, hatchets, a grindstone, muskets and musket bullets, another fowling piece, more powder and some shot. I tried to take some sheet lead but it was too heavy for me to carry over the ship's side.

I also loaded as many clothes as I could find, a spare sail, a hammock and some bedding.

As I rowed back to shore, I was worried in case the provisions I had left on the island would have been eaten by wild animals, but when I got back to my barricade, all I saw was a wild cat, not one of the ship's cats, who ran off as I approached, then stopped and sat down, staring at me.

I aimed my gun at her, but she didn't seem to mind, so I threw her a biscuit, which she smelt and ate before looking at me as if to say, "More please!"

But I could spare no more, and she ran off a few moment later.

I set to work making a tent out of the sail and some poles I cut for that purpose, and when it was ready I carried inside everything that I thought would be spoiled by sun or rain.

Next I piled up all the empty chests and caskets into a circle round my tent, to fortify it in case it was attacked by wild animals or, worse, savages.

I made a door from some boards, spread out some bedding and, with two pistols within easy reach, fell into a deep sleep.

I woke feeling refreshed and looking around me I laughed when I realized I must have had more guns and ammunition than any one person ever had.

Over the next few days, at low water, I swam back to the ship and ferried myself back on makeshift rafts loaded with ropes, twine, rigging, canvas, a barrel of wet gunpowder—anything I saw that I thought would be of use to me.

After five or six trips, I thought I had stripped her bare of all the provision she had aboard, but just as I was on the point of giving up, I found a great store of ship's biscuits, rum, sugar and flour. I wrapped everything in pieces of sail and took my parcels ashore.

Next day, I loaded cables, thick rope, pieces of iron and masts, intending to make a really strong raft, but as I approached the cove my overloaded raft capsized and my precious cargo was thrown into the water.

I thought it was all lost, but when the tide went out, I was able to retrieve the rope and some of the iron.

After that I went to the ship every day, taking care not to load too much onto my raft, and brought away everything I could carry.

By the time I had been on the island for thirteen days, I had been back to the ship eleven times.

"There can't be much left," I said to myself as I approached her for the twelfth time, but on that particular trip I discovered a locker containing three razors, scissors and a dozen or so good knives and forks. In another I came across thirty-six pounds in English and Brazilian coins.

"What good are these to a man in my situation?" I cried aloud, but nonetheless I wrapped everything up in canvas and began to think of making a raft to ferry myself ashore. But suddenly the wind began to rise. Knowing that the tide may be about to flood, I let myself into the water and swam ashore, almost weighted down by my most recent pickings.

By the time I got back to my little tent, a storm was blowing that raged well into the night.

Despite that, I managed to get a good night's sleep and next morning, when I looked out to sea, the ship was nowhere to be seen.

No-one could begin to imagine how pleased with

myself I was, having worked so hard to get everything off her that I thought could be useful to me.

I had been so busy that I had not had much time to worry about being attacked by wild animals or savages, but now, I decided, my tent would not give me much shelter from attack, so I decided to move.

But should I look for a cave or build a stronger tent?

Wherever I settled, the air must be good and the water nearby fresh. It should offer shade from the sun and safety from marauding men or beasts, and it must have a view of the sea in case, pray to God, a ship sailed into sight.

After a little searching, I found a little plain on the side of a hill. The plain was about 100 yards broad and twice as long, and was set beneath a slope so steep that nothing could approach me from above.

A small hollow was set in the rock, looking for all the world like the entrance to a cave.

The hill ran down to the sea, and because the plain was on the northwest side of the hill, I would be sheltered from the heat of the sun each day until evening.

Although there was no cave, I decided to pitch my tent in front of the hollow.

I set to work cutting down trees to make large stakes which I sharpened at both ends. That done, I drew a semicircle in the ground in front of the hollow and drove in the stakes in two lines, one in front of the other on either side of the line, each no more than six inches apart from the next and each sticking about five-and-half feet out of the ground.

Next I made sure that the ends sticking out of the ground were still sharp and then wove the heavy rope round the stakes, making a fence so strong and so sharp at the top that neither man nor beast could enter.

Rather than a door, I made a ladder to let myself in and out of my new home by climbing over the fence.

I carried all my supplies into the stockade and set to work building as large a tent as I could. I covered it with a tarpaulin and built a smaller one inside it for provisions that would be damaged by rain if they were left outside.

I put my hammock up and then began tunnelling into the hollow, carrying the earth, stones and rubble I dug out to beyond the stockade to make a terrace to surround my encampment. Now I had a space, which I thought of as a cave, behind my tent, which I could use as a cellar.

One day when I was busy doing all this there was a terrific storm. Thunderclaps roared overhead and great streaks of lightning flashed across the sky.

I was so afraid that if the lightning hit my gunpowder, my entire supply would be blown up, that I divided the entire supply—all 240 pounds of it—into more than 100 parcels and stored it in a dry barrel in my cave.

I took time off from my labours to go hunting and was delighted to find goats. At first I found it difficult to shoot them, so nimble were they on the rocks. But if I was on the rocks and they were grazing in the valleys, they paid no attention to me and I had time to aim properly.

The first one I shot was a she-goat feeding a young kid. When I picked the older animal up to carry her home on my shoulders, the kid followed me. I tried to feed it in the hope that I could tame her and milk her when she was old enough, but she would not eat and I was forced to kill her for the pot.

My new home built, I set about furnishing it, and although I had never tried my hand at carpentry before, with all the tools I had taken from the ship and the planks from my rafts, I made myself a table and chair.

I also felled more trees, and with the planks I hewed from their trunks, I put shelves along one side of my cave to store my tools and guns.

It was at this time that I decided to keep a diary of what I did every day and continued to do so until my supplies of ink started to run low.

Chapter Seven

I Get Used to Life

When I was not hard at work building or improving my encampment, I was learning more and more, not just about the island, but about myself.

I discovered pigeon-like birds that nested in holes in the rock and were good to eat.

I taught myself how to make a lamp, using tallow from the goats I killed and a wick made out of unravelled strands of rope.

Some old corn (that I shook from a bag that I was going to use to store things in) took root and grew as green barley. When I saw this, I cried because it reminded me of England.

One day when I was busy in the entrance to my cave, I heard a dreadful roar. The next moment, earth came crumbling down from the roof. Terrified that I was about to be engulfed, I ran for the ladder. As soon as I was on the other side of the fence, I realized that the island was being shaken by a violent earthquake.

As the earth rumbled, a dreadful hurricane began to blow, whipping up the sea to a frenzy of fury. The storm raged for three hours, and no sooner had it finished than it began to rain—not the gentle rain that washes England, but rain so violent that I had to cut a hole in the fortifications to let the water run out, otherwise my camp would have been flooded and all my possessions washed away.

As the rain fell, I realized that if earthquakes were common on my island, it may not be safe for me to go on living by the side of a hill, for the violent motions of the earth may have stirred an avalanche that would engulf me.

I decided I would have to build a hut in an open place that I could surround with a fortified wall, similar to the one around my cave.

The first thing that had to be done was to sharpen my tools. It took me a week to devise a method of turning the grindstone that I had taken from the ship, but I did it and spent two days sharpening every blade I had.

On the first day of May, as I walked along the beach pondering how to build my new dwelling, I came upon the remains of my ship, obviously whipped up from the sea bed by a violent tide and washed into shallow water a few yards from the beach.

When the tide went out, I found I could easily walk out to her. The insides were full of sand, but even so, here was timber and metal aplenty to build a hut.

I spent much of the weeks that followed pulling timbers and metal from the wreck, taking only as much time off as need be to hunt and fish in order to keep hunger at bay.

One day I caught a dolphin, which I dried in the sun and ate, and on another I spent so long in the woods hunting pigeons that by the time I went to the beach, the tide was in and I was unable to get to what was left of the vessel, which began to look like little more than a skeleton.

Everything that happened was faithfully recorded in my journal.

On June 16th, I caught a turtle and spent the next day cooking her. There were well over fifty eggs inside her. Looking back, I think that animal gave me some of the best meals of my life.

It was then that I fell ill.

On June 18th, it rained all day and I felt extremely cold. The next day I began to shiver as though I had been caught in a snowstorm, but on the night of June 20th, I fell into a fever.

I was certain that I was going to die, but I felt a little better the next day.

That, sadly, turned out to be a false dawn, for on June 23rd I felt as bad as ever and my head ached as though it had been beaten with a stout stick.

On June 26th, realizing that I had nothing to eat in my larder, I somehow found the strength to go to where the goats grazed. I managed to shoot one, which I hauled home with great difficulty and cooked, but the next day I was so weak I couldn't even rise from bed to quench my raging thirst.

I was so scared of death that I called out, "Lord, look upon me. Lord, pity me! Lord, have mercy upon me." Then I must have fallen into a deep sleep immediately afterwards, for the next thing I was wakening from a nightmare so horrible that even now I shiver when I think of it.

I drank some rum and water and ate some goat's flesh, which I cooked in the fire, and some turtle's eggs. I tried to walk, but was still so weak that I had to sit down when I was just a few yards from my stockade.

When I got back to my hammock, I drank some rum and then fell asleep.

I didn't waken until three o'clock the next day, or it could even have been the day after that!

Whichever it was, I felt so much better that the next day I was strong enough to go hunting and bagged some sea birds and a goose of some sort.

I continued to get better, but did not recover my full strength until well into July.

So thankful was I to God for making me well, for I was sure that without Him I would have died, I began to read my Bible regularly. I also began to pray devoutly, asking Him to forgive me for my sins.

I started to feel so well that I decided to embark on a survey of the entire island. I had been on the island for ten months by now, and had not wandered far from my camp. Now I began to venture farther and farther.

Farther up the creek where I had landed my rafts, I discovered meadows where tobacco and wild sugar cane grew—plants that I knew well from my days in Brazil. Beyond the meadows, the country became woody, and there I found fruit trees, melons and vines heavy with grapes.

I spent the night in the woods, sleeping in the branches of a tree in case animals prowled about the place at night.

Next morning, I walked on a ridge of hills on the south and north of me, until I came to an opening where the country fell away to the west. A little spring gurgled out from the side of a hill and the whole country was fresh and green.

As I walked through groves of citrus trees, I picked limes that I squeezed into water, which made it a very refreshing drink.

I decided to lay in stores of fruit for the rainy season, which I knew to be fast approaching, and gathered great armfuls of lemons, limes and grapes, which I left in piles, resolving to return for them with sacks. But when I did so, I found that the many of the grapes had been trampled on and scattered in all directions, obviously by some wild creatures. Many of grapes that had survived had been crushed by their own weight. So I hung them on branches to dry in the sun.

Later, as I made my way home, my sacks bursting with lemons, limes and grapes dried into raisins, I was as proud as any Lord of the Manor when he takes in his harvest.

I considered building my new house in this green paradise, but it was out of sight of the sea and to have done so would have been admitting to myself that I would never get off the island. But I did set about creating a bower for myself there, and I built a fence around it.

As I lay there one night, I smiled at a thought that crossed my mind—I now had a seaside house and a country house.

Shortly after this, it started to rain and I was forced to return to my fort. It poured from August 14th for two weeks.

Unable to go out, apart from once when I killed a goat, I worked at enlarging my cellar, and eventually it was so large that I made a door into it from beyond my fence.

It was during these weeks that one of the cats returned with three kittens—which came as a surprise as it had been assumed that both the ship's cats were female!

So many cats bred from these and future kittens that they became such pests that years later I was forced to kill them like vermin.

A few weeks after the rains stopped, I realized that it was September 30th.

I had been on my island for a year.

I fasted all day and resolved that every seventh day from then on I would observe as the Sabbath.

A little later, my ink supplies began to run low and I resolved to write down only the most memorable events that happened to me.

Chapter Eight

I Am Seldom Idle

Having now been on the island for twelve months, I became aware that the year could be divided into rainy and dry seasons, and I decided to plant the corn and rice that I had taken from the ship.

Fortunately I didn't plant it all, for my first attempt came to nothing as I mistimed my sowing.

I sowed a second crop, which yielded some grain, enough for me to sow even more during the next seed time, and as the years passed I confidently sowed and harvested two times a year.

When I returned to my bower for the first time, I was delighted to find that some of the stakes that I had used to fence it in had taken root and had grown so many leaves that there was enough shade for me to spend all the hot dry season there.

I taught myself how to make baskets from twigs that I cut and dried in the sun.

After so long on the island, I realized that I wanted for very little. All I needed were some more bottles or vessels to hold liquid in, some small pots and a small kettle, the ones that I had being designed to serve a ship's crew, and a pipe, my old one being little better than useless.

Nothing near to where I lived, either on the coast or

in my bower, offered itself to suit any of these purposes, so I decided to explore more of the island.

I called my dog and, taking my gun, a hatchet, powder and shot, some ship's biscuit and a great bunch of raisins, I set out.

When I reached a point far beyond my bower, I looked out to sea and spied land some twenty leagues off, but I had no way of knowing if it was Spanish territory or inhabited by savages. If it was Spanish, then surely a ship would pass sooner or later. If it was inhabited by savages, then it was just as well that I had been washed ashore where I was and not there, or else I would surely have been killed and probably eaten by now.

As I walked on, I found myself on a part of the island that was much more pleasant than where I lived. There were open, sweet fields adorned with flowers and grass, and there were woods of fine trees. So many parrots glided from branch to branch that I managed to bring one down to take home, intending to teach it to speak.

As I came to the seashore, I found it covered with turtles and many, many more birds than there were on my side of the island.

Beautiful though this place was, I was not tempted to move there, for I had become so used to my present living arrangements that I had come to think of my fort, my cave and my bower as home.

I decided to return by another route, but I became so scared of becoming lost in a large valley that I found myself in that I made my way back the way I had come.

As we went, my dog startled a young kid and was on the point of killing it when I came to its rescue, for I had been thinking about trying to build up a herd of tame goats to slaughter when my shot and powder eventually ran out. Here was a fine young male. If, later, I could catch a young nanny, I would be lucky.

Making a lead for it from the twine that I always carried, I led the animal home to my bower where I left him and set off for the coast.

I was glad to be home again and set to work making a cage for my parrot, but after a week I set off for my bower again to tend for my kid.

I was horrified to find him on the brink of starvation for I had thought there was enough grazing in my bower for him. I cut him something to munch on, and when I went to make my way home, he followed me all the way like a dog, and from then on would rarely let me out of his sight. But it was to be many years before my plans to become a goatherd came to anything.

Shortly afterwards, September 30th came round again. I had been on the island for two years, and the prospect of being saved seemed as remote now as it was on the day that I had been washed ashore.

* * *

The years passed. I continued to plant my crops and dry my raisins, I went shooting and I started a project that was to keep me busy for day after day, week after week, month after month—hollowing out a tree trunk to make a canoe.

My first attempt came to nothing, for the tree I cut for the purpose was far too large for me to get to the water. But I had learned my lesson, and I set to work on a much smaller tree trunk.

Having been on the island for so long, my clothes had long since started to decay. The contents of the seamen's chests kept me attired, but when these garments in turn became useless, I made myself a sort of suit and a cap from goatskins.

I also spent a great deal of time making myself an umbrella to provide some shade when I was walking in the sun, and as an amusement I tried to teach Poll, my parrot, to speak but, despite my labours, she refused to say as much as one word.

By the time I was in my sixth year on the island, my canoe was at last ready. I fitted her with a sail, stocked her with provisions and set off to sail round the island.

Rocks on the far side of the island forced me much farther out to sea than I wanted to go, and when I landed on the first day, I climbed a hill and observed the way that the currents flowed around the coast. Armed with this knowledge, I took to sea again but found myself being swept farther and farther away from the land.

No matter how hard I paddled, the distance between me and the island grew greater and greater. I was terrified in case it vanished from view altogether, for without a compass I would have no way of knowing how to get back to it.

Just when I thought all was lost, a breeze rose. I

raised my sail and managed to steer myself towards the island. I landed on the northern shore, exactly opposite to the point from where I had started. I fell on my knees and thanked God for my safe deliverance.

But how to get home? I was scared of going back to sea again, but I did not want to abandon my boat, so I decided to make my way westward, keeping to shallow coastal waters. But after paddling against the current for about three miles, I reached a small inlet in which I tied up my boat.

That done, with gun in one hand and umbrella in the other, I set out to walk for home. I was pleasantly surprised when, in the early evening, I reached my bower. Exhausted by my long walk in the blazing sun, I clambered over the fence, laid down in the shade and fell into a deep sleep.

I was astonished to be wakened by someone calling my name. "Robin Crusoe! Poor Robin Crusoe! Where are you, Robin Crusoe?"

Chapter Nine

I Find a Footprint

I looked around me, so startled that my heart was thumping. There was no-one to be seen. A few seconds later the voice spoke again, and it was only then that I realized that it was Poll, my parrot. All those hours teaching her to talk had not been wasted after all.

I decided that I had had enough of rambling for the time being, and although I would have liked to have my boat with me, having taken so long to make it and to get it down to the sea, I decided that it could stay where it was.

I made my mind up to improve my carpentry skills and to find some way of making pots. It took me a long time, but eventually I managed to make a wheel on which to turn wet clay, from which I even managed to make myself a pipe!

I also practised making baskets and became better and better at it.

The months turned to years, and by the time I had been on the island for ten years, I was an excellent woodworker, a fair potter and a gifted basketmaker.

It was now that I realized that my supply of powder and shot was getting less and less, and I started to ponder on how I should kill goats when my ammunition ran out completely.

I decided to set some traps and was delighted one morning to find an old nanny goat in one and three kids—two females and a male—in another.

I let the old goat go, and after I had tied the three youngsters together, I led them home. That done, I set to work to build an enclosure for them in an open meadow, with enough grazing and water to keep them happy. By the time I had finished, I had fenced in an area 150 yards long and 100 yards broad, and I set my three goats free in it.

Within a year, my flock had risen in number to twelve, and a year later I had forty-three of them. I now had goat's flesh to eat, their milk to drink and, once I had taught myself the necessary arts of the dairy, butter and cheese.

Sometimes when I dined I imagined myself king of all I surveyed, dining well and attended by my servants, Poll, my dog (who was now old and half-mad) and two cats who had come to live with me.

"But no man looks less like a king," I said to myself one day as I walked along the beach. My crown was a large, goatskin cap with a flap hanging down the back to keep the sun off my neck in fine weather and the water from running down my back when it rained.

My robes were a short jacket, also of goatskin, with skirts reaching to the thighs. And to round off my regal outfit, I was wearing goatskin breeches and pieces of hide wrapped round my feet to serve as shoes.Hanging from the belt around my waist were a saw and a hatchet, and on the strip of goatskin that ran over my shoulder and down my chest, there were two pouches, one for my powder and another for my shot.

I carried a basket on my back, a gun over my shoulder, and in my hand I held the umbrella that I had made to shade me from the sun.

Suddenly I was stopped dead in my tracks when I saw a footprint in the sand. I looked all around, but there was no-one to be seen. I ran up and down the beach, shouting, but no-one answered my call. Terrified in case I was about to be attacked by savages, I ran back to my fort, and when I got there I was so scared that I can't, even now, remember if I used the ladder or the hole in the rock to enter it.

I slept not at all that night, cowering in terror and expecting to find myself under siege from who knows what at any moment.

I thought it may be the devil, having taken on some sort of human form, come to claim my soul.

I considered the idea that it may have been put there by God to scare me as a punishment for my sins.

Eventually I decided that the footprint must have been made by someone who had wandered out to sea in a canoe from the far-off mainland and been swept to my island by the wind or currents.

For three days I was too scared to move, but when the provisions I had in my fort started to run out, I was forced to venture out.

Gradually my courage returned, and I became brave enough to go to my enclosure to milk my goats. It was while I was doing this that the thought struck me that maybe the footprint was one of my own. The more I thought of it, the more I became convinced that that was the case.

Plucking up my courage, I made my way back to the footprint, but when I measured my own foot against it, it was obvious that the print had been made by someone else.

It took some time for me to get used to the idea that either someone had visited the island or that some part of it that I had not yet visited was inhabited.

But eventually things returned to normal, and I began to move about more or less with the same sense of freedom that I had had before.

But one day, when I was looking out to sea from halfway up a hill, I saw what seemed to be a boat, sailing away from the island. I watched until it had vanished from sight before making my way to the part of the island from which, if the current had behaved as I would have expected it to, the boat would have set out.

Imagine my horror at what I saw when I reached that beach, for the area was littered with human bones—skulls, hands and feet—all scattered around a fire-blackened pit. The horror of what must have happened slowly dawned on me.

Whoever had lit the fire, had cooked and eaten the poor souls thrown into it.

My island had been visited by cannibals!

For the next few years I scarcely left my fort or my bower, and wherever I went I carried guns with me, although I was cautious about firing them in case the sound caught the unwelcome attention of some unseen presence on the island. Thankfully, because I had had the foresight to build up my herd of goats, I no longer needed to hunt.

The thought of cannibalism upset me so much that I made up my mind to catch one of these savages if the opportunity ever presented itself.

My chance came eighteen months later, when I was surprised one morning to see five canoes pulled up onto the beach not far from my fort.

There was no sign of anyone near them, but when I climbed to the top of my fence to get a better view, I saw thirty naked savages dancing around a fire that they had made farther along the beach.

Keeping my head down as far as possible, I saw them stop dancing and drag two miserable captives from one of the canoes.

As soon as they were on the beach, one of the savages knocked one of the pair to the sand with a stout club. No sooner was he on the ground than the others fell upon him and started to cut the flesh from his bones, throwing it on their fire.

The other victim was left standing on his own while the savages concentrated on their fiendish work. Obviously sensing a chance of freedom, he sprinted along the beach, directly towards me.

It came to me that I must save the poor fellow's life,

not only because it was my Christian duty to do so but also because it had been many years since I had enjoyed the luxury of a servant.

By now two of the savages were chasing the poor fellow.

Picking up my guns, I ran from my fort into the undergrowth and from there onto the beach, where I found I was positioned between the pursued and the pursuers, now far from the others.

I called on the prey to come to me, and as he did so I advanced slowly towards his chasers, who had stopped in their tracks. The first I hit with the stock of my musket. As he fell, I noticed that his companion had taken a bow and arrow from his shoulders and was already aiming it at me.

One shot from my gun killed him instantly.

By this time, the man who had fled was by my side, staring in astonishment at my gun, obviously baffled by how such a thing could have killed a man from so far off.

He fell to his knees, kissing my feet, then picked up my right foot and put it on his head, as if to say, "I am your slave forever."

I pulled him to his feet, and we walked towards the man whom I had struck with my gun. As we approached, I raised my gun, but my savage pointed at my sword and then to himself. Understanding his meaning, I gave it to him and watched as with one mighty blow he cut the fellow's head off. He picked it up by the hair and laid it at my feet along with the sword.

I pointed in the direction of my fort and indicated that he should follow me there, but the savage pointed at the two bodies and then into the distance where their companions, obviously unaware of what had happened, were still dancing round the fire.

I understood that my savage wanted to bury the bodies so that they would not be found by their fellow cannibals.

I nodded, and he set to work. When he was finished, he followed me to my fort, now so well camouflaged by trees and shrubs that even if the savages came looking for their prisoner they would not have found him.

My savage was a handsome fellow, with strong, straight limbs, tall and well shaped. He was, I reckoned, about twenty-six years of age. I poured him some milk and showed him how to drink it, and then I taught him how to dip bread in the milk to soften it before he ate it.

Next, I made him know his name, which was to be "Friday", which was the day of the week, and then my name, which was to be "Master". I kept him with me all that night, and the next morning we went to see if his captors had left the island. The sight that met our eyes was dreadful.

The area was covered with human bones and pieces of fire-blackened flesh. The sand was dyed red by the blood that had flowed.

Once we had made sure that Friday's captors had all gone, I set the fellow to work gathering all the remains together, and, that done, we lit a fire and burned them all to ashes.

We went back to my fort, where I gave my man Friday a pair of linen drawers, for he was quite naked, and then I set to work making him a goatskin jerkin and a hareskin cap.

The next thing to be done was to decide where he was to live. It was out of the question that he should stay within the fort—what servant lives so close to his master—so I built him a tent in the gap between the two walls of my fort, and he seemed very content to be there.

Chapter Ten

My Servant Settles In

Now that I had two mouths to feed, I realized that
I would have to clear more ground to grow enough
corn to feed two people. Once I had selected the spot
and shown him what to do, Friday set to work quite
cheerfully, and when the ground was cleared, I showed
him how to erect a fence around it.

And so began the happiest year of my life on the
island. Never was there a more faithful, loving or
sincere servant than Friday. Every task I set him, he
did willingly, and once he had learned some English,
it was a joy to have someone to talk to after having
been on my own for so long.

I taught my man to shoot, which he came to do
extremely well.

I taught him how to milk the goats and make butter
and cheese.

I showed him how to make baskets.

In fact, I taught him everything that I had myself
had to learn.

When I told him how I had come to be on the island,
he begged to be shown the remains of the ship, which
still lay where they had been washed ashore.

When he saw them, he said, "Me see such boat like
come to place at my nation."

I was puzzled by this at first, but as I questioned him I learned that a ship had been wrecked on the rocks off the mainland some years before, and Friday and some other savages had rescued seventeen white men from the vessel.

"What happened to them?" I asked.

"They live, they dwell at my nation."

It turned out that for four years the white men had lived with the savages.

"Haven't they been eaten?" I asked.

"No!" Friday replied. "They make brother with them."

It was some time after this, when we were at the top of a hill one very clear day, that Friday looked out to sea and cried, "Oh joy! Oh glad! There see my country. There my nation."

He sounded so happy to see his own land again that I took him round to the other side of the island where my old boat lay and showed it to him.

"Is that big enough to carry us to your nation?" I asked.

Friday shook his head.

A few days later I led him to the place where, long before, I had made the boat that I been unable to get to the water because of its bulk. As Friday looked at the rotting remains, I asked him if a vessel that size would be big enough.

He nodded. "Would carry enough vittle, drink, bread," he said.

"Very well," I said, "let's set to work and build another one."

Friday selected a tree and felled it. He wanted to burn out the inside, as was the custom with his people, but after I showed him how to use an axe, he managed the job very well.

Once the inside was finished, we rolled her to the water, which took near on two weeks. There, I fitted her with a mast fashioned from a tall, slender cedar tree and a sail made from old pieces of canvas that I had taken from my wreck so many years before.

While I was sewing the sails, Friday was happy to dig a little dock for our boat, just deep enough to give our vessel water to float in. And then, when the tide was out, we made a dam across the end of it to keep the sea water out. Next, we covered her with branches to keep the rain off, and now there was nothing more to be done but wait until November or December came around, for I thought that if we sailed during these months, we would have a good chance of reaching the mainland.

Chapter Eleven

We Fight a Battle

We started to lay in stores for the journey, and one day when I had sent Friday to the seashore to get a tortoise or turtle, he returned breathless and almost flew over the outer wall of my fort, so anxious was he to tell me his news.

"Oh, Master," he panted, "out there—one, two, three canoe."

"Well then, Friday," I said, pouring him a tot of rum to calm him, "we must be prepared to fight if necessary."

We went up the hill to my vantage point, where I counted twenty-one savages and three prisoners, as well as the three canoes.

We ran back to the fort to collect our swords and to arm ourselves with a pistol apiece to stick in our belts and three guns each to carry on our shoulders. I put a small bottle of rum in my pocket and handed Friday two large bags, one of shot and the other of ammunition.

So armed, we made our way into the woods, where we crept as close to the edge as we dared without risking being seen. After a few minutes, I pointed to a large tree just where the beach met the woods and whispered to Friday to crawl to it and tell me what he saw on his return. He was not gone long.

"Master," he said, "two prisoner dead. Other I know. He one live with us. White man!"

We watched as nineteen of the savages sat huddled together while the other two went to butcher the white man. There was no time to lose.

We fired our muskets at the savages, Friday killing two and injuring three more, while I killed one and injured two.

Our second volley, this time using small bullets, killed two but injured so many more that they ran about yelling and screaming.

"Now, Friday!" I shouted.

We ran out of the wood towards the prisoner. The two savages who had been about to kill him had fled to their canoes along with three others.

While I cut the prisoner free, Friday fired at the men in the canoe, again killing two and injuring the third.

"What are you?" I asked the man (whom I had freed) in Portuguese.

"Christianus," he answered in Latin, but his voice was so weak I could hardly hear him.

I pulled the rum from my pocket and handed it to him.

"Where are you from?" I asked as he gulped down a great mouthful of the liquor.

"Spain," he replied.

"If you have any strength left," I said, "you must help us fight."

And without waiting for an answer, I thrust a gun and a sword into his hands.

The effect was astonishing. He ran towards the enemy and within an instant had cut two of them down.

I called on Friday to bring me another gun, and as I sat loading it I watched the Spaniard fight a giant of a savage. Just when it looked as if my friend was about to be hacked to death, he drew the gun from his belt and shot the fellow through the chest.

Friday meanwhile had killed another three of the savages with his hatchet, and the Spaniard, having exhausted his powder and ammunition, came to me to ask for another weapon.

The moment I thrust a freshly loaded fowling piece into his hands, he ran off in pursuit of two savages, wounding them both with his gunshot. Somehow they still had the strength to dash into the wood, but a few moments later one of them was back on the beach with Friday hot on his heels.

"One dead!" my man called, but before he could kill the second, the savage splashed into the sea and swam out to one of the canoes, where the only savages now left alive were getting ready to row away.

I ran into the water to one of the other canoes, calling on Friday to follow me, and when I jumped into it, I was amazed to find another prisoner, a savage by the look of him, lying in the bottom, bound hand and foot.

I had cut the poor fellow free and was giving him a dram of rum when Friday reached us. I could hardly believe my eyes when my man began to jump up and down, embraced the man and kissed him time and time again.

It was some time before my man could speak, and when I asked him what the matter was, he told me that the savage was his father.

I told Friday to go back to the shore where the Spaniard, now exhausted by his efforts, lay slumped on the beach. I watched my man lift him onto his shoulders and carry him back to the canoe.

That done, I returned to the shore to pick up our guns and swords, and let Friday row the canoe back to the beach near my fort while I made my way there on foot.

As I approached, I was surprised to see my man running towards me.

"Where are you going?" I asked.

"Go fetch more boat," he replied.

When I reached my beach, the two men were lying on the sand, obviously too tired to make it to my fort. So I set to work to make a kind of wheelbarrow, and when Friday came back he sat his father and the Spaniard in it and pushed it up the hill to my fort.

I decided that my guests should lodge outside the fort and erected a tent for them between the outside fence and a grove of trees that I had planted a little way off. When I had covered it with branches and fitted it out with rice straw and blankets, it did the two men very well indeed.

I now had three subjects, all of whom owed me their lives and would, no doubt, have lain them down for me had I asked them to.

And it amused me that while I was a Protestant and had instructed Friday in that religion, his father was a pagan cannibal and the Spaniard a Catholic. As fair a mix of religions as would be found in kingdoms many times the size of mine.

Chapter Twelve

My Guests Settle In

Once I had provided my two guests with shelter and bedding, I began to think that perhaps, as a good host, I ought to give them something to eat. I sent Friday to kill a goat, a tender young one, and when he had carried out my instructions, I skinned it and cut the meat into joints. One of these I gave to Friday and told him to boil it and make a stew for our guests.

When the stew was bubbling away, I added some barley and rice, and when the meal was cooked, I carried the pot to the tent we had made for Friday's father and the Spaniard.

"Bring a table," I turned and said to Friday, who was, as usual, walking a little way behind me, as any servant should. "The small round one will do nicely."

The table was one I had made many years before when I was still learning the art of carpentry. I had very little use for it now in my quarters, but it was perfectly adequate for my guests.

When Friday had brought the table and set the stew upon it, I called his father and the Spaniard from their tent where they were asleep.

I decided to eat with them, to cheer them up and encourage them as best I could. Friday was my interpreter for the Spaniard, who was one of the band of Europeans who had lived among Friday's people for many years, spoke the language of the savages very well.

"Do you think your people will return?" I asked Friday's father.

The old savage shook his head. "They will be too scared by the way you killed so many of them with your magic that they will not dare."

"And even if they did," I thought to myself, "now that there are four of us and enough weapons for us all, we would be more than a match for ten times our number."

When the meal was finished, I told Friday to return to the beach to collect any firearms that we may have left behind and to bury the dead.

As the days passed, I talked more and more to the Spaniard, and one day he told me that there were sixteen of his fellow countrymen living among the savages on the mainland and that they would do anything to escape and sail to the colonies in America.

"Perhaps," I said to him, "now there are four of us, we could build another boat, one big enough for such a voyage. But can they all be trusted?" I asked, remembering what I knew about the Spanish and their Inquisition—that dreadful time when heretics were tortured until they recanted their sins, only, more often than not, to be burned at the stake. "I'd rather be eaten by savages than fall foul of the Inquisition!" I said

"Don't worry," the Spaniard reassured me. "I'll make sure every one of them swears absolute loyalty to you before we leave the mainland. And if any man refuses, he'll have me to reckon with."

So assured, I decided that a new boat should be built, and as we walked through the woods, I selected several trees to be felled and cut into planks to build a vessel large enough to hold so many people.

I set Friday and his father to work chopping down the trees and asked the Spaniard to supervise them, showing him planks that I had hewn from trees myself many years before when I had been alone on the island.

"We'll need dozens like these," I said, pointing to a large piece of oak, thirty-five feet long, two feet broad and a good four inches thick.

"When do you plan to sail?" he asked me, and when I told him that I hoped to go as soon as the boat was ready, with luck within a few weeks, he advised me to delay for at least six months.

"We'll need to have plenty of provisions to feed so many more mouths on a long voyage," he said.

He was right. If our numbers were to be swelled to twenty, we would need a great deal more food than I had in my storehouse.

The first thing to be done was to increase the number of tame goats in my herd to supply us with meat, milk, cheese and butter. I sent Friday and the Spaniard out one day to capture as many kid goats as possible, for the younger the goat, the easier it was to tame.

The method was simple. When they saw a mother goat surrounded by kids, they shot the mother and as her young stood round her, bleating, they tethered them and led them back to the enclosure. By doing this, we added twenty kids to my breeding herd. The mothers we skinned and dried their meat in the sun.

Fortunately, it was the time of year when the vines were heavy with grapes. I told Friday and his father to pick as many bunches as they could and hang them in the sun. By the time they had turned to raisins, there was enough to fill eighty barrels—had we had that many.

Next we took in the harvest. We cut down the corn and rice and threshed it, and by the time we had finished we had 220 bushels of both—more than enough to feed all those expected on the island for our voyage. The harvest in, we set to work making wicker baskets in which to keep our grain. The Spaniard proved extremely good at this, after I had shown him how to do it.

When all this had been done, it was time to go to the mainland to round up the Spaniards. I decided to send Friday's father and the Spaniard on ahead, and they duly set off, but not before I had instructed the Spaniard to make all those he intended to bring back swear an oath promising that they would in no way injure, fight or attack me or Friday when they arrived here.

They left in one of the canoes the savages had come to the island in, both armed with a musket, powder and balls.

"Only fire them in an emergency," I said, for although I had learned to make most of the things I needed, powder and ammunition were not among them.

I also gave them enough bread and dried grapes to feed them and whomever they brought back for much longer than I was sure the return voyage would take.

Just before they set off, on a fine October morning, I think the 26th October, we decided on a signal that they should make before they landed on their return. That done, they took to the water, a fine wind behind them. Friday and I watched until they were little more than dots in the ocean, and then we returned to my fort to await their return.

Chapter Thirteen

A Ship Sails In

It was eight days later when a strange thing happened, something so unexpected that never in a thousand years could I have thought such a thing would occur.

I was fast asleep one morning when I was awakened by Friday shouting, "Master, Master! They are come! They are come!"

I jumped up and, as soon as I had pulled on some clothes, ran through the trees to a point where I could see the ocean. There was something in the way Friday had shouted that had so surprised me that I had left my home without carrying a gun with me, which was most unusual, for I cannot recall the last time I had done such a thing.

When I looked out to sea, I saw a longboat about a league and a half away, sailing towards the shore.

It seemed not to be coming from the direction where the mainland lay but from the southernmost point of the island. I called Friday and told him to lie low, for if I was right, this was not the Spaniard and Friday's father.

I ran to the top of the hill to get a better view, and no sooner had I reached the summit than I saw a large ship lying at anchor, south-southeast. Judging from her rigging and shape, I took her to be an English vessel, and as the first boat I had seen drew nearer, I could plainly see it was an English longboat.

I didn't know what to think. The sight of an English ship, no doubt with an English crew aboard, sent a surge of joy coursing through my veins. At the same time, I was suspicious. What was an English ship doing in these waters? If I had been told that a ship were to sail into view, I would have assumed that she would be Spanish or Portuguese, for England had no trade in this part of the world.

"Perhaps," I said to myself, "she's been blown off course." But no sooner had the thought come to mind than I realized that there had been no storm.

If I was right, and it was an English ship, then she must be up to no good, and rather than go and welcome them ashore, Friday and I should keep out of sight.

I watched the boat near the island, the crew obviously looking for a suitable place to land. For a moment, it looked as if they were going to sail up the creek where I had landed my rafts all those years before when I had been shipwrecked.

Had they done so, they might have seen something to suggest that the island was not uninhabited, as I was sure they thought it was. But happily they passed by and beached their boat about half a mile from where I was watching.

Eleven men, most probably English by the look of them, came ashore. Three of them were bound, plainly prisoners, and one of these three seemed to be pleading desperately with his captors.

"Oh, Master," whispered Friday, "you see white man eat prisoner as well as savage man."

"No!" I hissed. "I'm afraid that the three may be about to be murdered, but you may be sure that they will not be eaten."

A chill ran through my veins as I watched one of the sailors raise his cutlass. I expected at any moment to see it sweep through the air, killing one, then another, then the third prisoner.

But the man wielding the sword seemed content to taunt his captives rather than slaughter them—at least for the time being. After a few minutes, the prisoners were untied, but they made no effort to escape, not even when their captors went off to explore the island, leaving the three wretches sitting on the beach, staring about them like men in despair.

The way they hung their heads reminded me of my own agony when I had first been washed ashore and had been so scared that I had spent the first night in a tree in case I was devoured by wild animals.

Friday and I stayed where we were, watching the tide go out, leaving the boat high and dry so that when the men returned she was sitting on soft, oozy sand.

I heard one of them call out a name, and a moment later two men stood up in the boat. I could tell from the bottles that they were both clutching that they had been drinking brandy, and from the way they were standing, they had been drinking too much of it!

"Fools!" someone shouted, running across the beach to the boat. "I told you to keep watch."

I didn't hear what the reply was, but I watched the sailors put their shoulders to the boat and try to push her towards the water.

"Let her be, Jack," another cried. "She'll float on the next tide."

Friday and I had hardly stirred while all this had been happening, but knowing that we had ten hours until the tide came in, I signalled him to follow me back to the fort, being careful to keep well out of sight. As I approached it, I was thankful at how well camouflaged it was now, with well over twenty-five years of growth surrounding it. Once there, we armed ourselves with muskets and fowling pieces and, so armed, made our way back to our vantage point.

I had intended to wait until dark, when the tide would next rise, to make my attempt to free the prisoners, but as we neared the beach to see how things lay, I saw that the captors, obviously unused to the heat of the early afternoon sun and encouraged by drinking too much brandy, had all fallen asleep.

Their three prisoners were sitting with their backs to us in the shade of a large tree about a quarter of a mile along the beach.

We must have cut strange figures, Friday and I, as we approached them. I was wearing a long goatskin coat and a large cap, with two pistols and my knife tucked in my belt and a gun on each shoulder. Friday, a little distance behind me, was not quite so strikingly dressed but, nonetheless, must have looked quite formidable.

"What are you, gentlemen?" I called in Spanish when I was within earshot.

They spun round, looks of utter astonishment on their faces when they saw who had called.

"Don't be alarmed, gentlemen," I said, this time in English. "You have, in me, a friend."

Chapter Fourteen

We Free the Prisoners

"He must have come from heaven," I heard one of the men say gravely.

"All help is from heaven," I said, and went on to tell them what I had seen.

One of the men, tears running down his face and trembling like a jellyfish, looked at me and said, "Am I talking to God or a man? Is it a real man or an angel?"

"If God had sent an angel to help you, do you not think he would have come better clothed than I? And would an angel need guns?"

The men relaxed a little.

"I am an Englishman, like you," I said, "come to assist you in your plight, my servant and I."

"You see that ship there?" one of the men said, pointing out to sea.

I nodded.

"I am her commander, or was until my men mutinied," he went on. "This is my mate, and this a passenger we had aboard." He nodded at the other two in turn as he spoke.

"My men threatened to kill us, but when this place came into view they decided to leave us here to perish, believing it to be uninhabited."

"Are they all asleep?" I asked.

"Every man jack of them," the mate said. "But speak softly, sir, for if they wake and find you here, they will surely murder us all."

"Are they armed? With firearms?"

"They have two guns, that's all," the captain said, eyeing the weapons that Friday and I carried.

"Well then," I said, "leave the rest to me. If they are all asleep, it will be an easy matter to kill them. Silently," I added, taking the knife from my belt. "Or we could take them prisoner."

"They don't all deserve to die," said the captain. "The two ringleaders are black-hearted dogs, but as for the others, I think they and the rest of the crew still aboard the ship would return to their duties."

"Which two are they?" I asked.

"I can't tell from here," said the captain.

"In that case," I said, "let us make our way into the woods, in case they awake, to make plans."

When we were safely out of sight and hearing of the mutineers, I said to the captain, "I'll make sure you get your freedom on two conditions … "

"We'll do anything," the captain interrupted. "If we get back to the ship, you shall take over command, if that's what you want, and we will sail to any part of the world that you wish."

"Aye!" cried the mate and passenger with one voice.

"That's just as it should be," I said. "Now, my conditions are, first, that while you are on this island I have absolute authority. You will do whatever I say. Although I shall, of course, ask your opinion if need be."

They all nodded.

"And, secondly, that if the ship is recovered, you will carry me and my man to England, free."

Again, they nodded.

"If we succeed, sir," the captain said, "we will owe you our lives and will acknowledge that fact for as long as we shall live."

I gave him and his companions guns, powder and ball.

"What do you think we should do?" I asked, as we made our way back to where some of the men were asleep.

"As I said, I am happy to be led by you," the captain said.

"Let us be guided by God," I said. "Let us fire a volley upon them as they lie. Those that are not killed we will ask to follow us. God will guide the direction of the shot."

"I don't want to kill anyone without due cause," said the captain, "but those two I mentioned are troublemakers."

As he spoke, two of the men stirred and started to get to their feet.

"Are these the two?" I asked.

The captain shook his head.

"Well then," I said, "you can let them escape. But if they do, and they somehow help their fellows to get away, it will be your fault."

The captain raised the firearm that I had given him, but before he could shoot, the mate and the passenger fired their weapons.

One of the men fell dead and the other was obviously badly wounded. The captain went to where the stricken man stood, clutching his wound.

"It's too late to cry for help now," he said, and with that knocked him to the ground with the stock of his musket so powerfully that the man must have died instantly.

By this time, three of the others had stirred, wakened by the gunshot, and when they saw the danger that they were in, they fell to their knees and pleaded for mercy.

"We'll be faithful to you, sir," one of them sobbed. "Please don't kill us."

"We'll help you get the ship back and sail it back to Jamaica," wailed another.

The captain looked at me.

"I leave it to you," I said. "But if you decide to let them live, I insist that they are bound hand and foot while they remain on the island."

While the men were being bound, I sent Friday and the mate to tie up the boat and bring her oars and sail back to me.

It was then that the other mutineers ran to where the rest of us were standing and, seeing the two dead bodies and their three fellow conspirators now securely bound, surrendered and allowed themselves to be tied up.

Our victory was complete.

It was only now that the captain asked how I came to be on the island. He listened, wide-eyed, as I told him my story and how I had used what I could take from my wrecked ship along with the resources of the island to furnish myself with provisions and ammunition.

It must have seemed to him that I had been put on the island by God so that his life might be saved, for as he listened he began to weep and was unable to speak until his tears had dried.

When he had recovered, I led him and his two men, the mate having by now returned with Friday, to my fort where I gave them something to eat and drink.

When they saw my castle and how I had so cleverly furnished it and hidden it from view, they were amazed. The little grove of trees I had planted beyond the outer wall was now a thick wood, so thick that the only way through it was by a path that I had cut in the undergrowth.

"I also have a bower where I spend a great deal of time," I said.

And when I described it to him, he said, "This, sir, I must see."

"Indeed you shall, sir," I said, "but only after we have worked out a way for you to get your ship back."

"Impossible," he cried.

"Why, sir?" I wanted to know.

"Because there are still twenty-six men on board," he replied, "and having mutinied they are hardly likely to help me sail my ship back to England or the colonies, for there they would surely be hanged."

Chapter Fifteen

More Mutineers Arrive
on the Island

As I sat there, trying to think of a way to draw the men aboard into some sort of trap while at the same time stopping them capturing and, no doubt, killing us all, it occurred to me that they must surely by now be wondering what had happened to their comrades ashore and that it could only be a matter of time before they sent a boat to the island.

When I put this to the captain, he agreed.

"In that case, sir," I said, "we must hole the boat that Friday has just tied up, so that they do not take her back with them. And we must take any provisions off her."

We made our way back to the beach and the longboat and took some firearms that we found in her, along with a bottle of brandy and another of rum, some ship's biscuits, a horn of powder, a huge lump of sugar, and some canvas. Everything was all very welcome to me, especially the brandy and the sugar, neither of which I had tasted for many years.

When all this had been taken to the shore, we knocked a great hole in the bottom of the boat so that, should a rescue party arrive, they could not take the boat with them when they left and we should then have the use of it, should we still be alive.

If I had been completely honest, I would have told the captain that I thought it extremely unlikely that we would ever take the ship, but at least we could easily repair the holed boat and sail it to the Leeward Islands, stopping off on the way to pick up the Spaniard and his compatriots and Friday's father, who must by now be on the mainland.

While we were at work, we heard a gun being fired from the ship, and when we turned to look out to sea, we saw a flag being waved, no doubt a signal for the men, who had escorted the captain, the mate and the passenger to the island, to return to the ship.

Some time later we saw a boat being lowered into the water. Obviously, there having been no response to the signal, some of the crew were coming to investigate.

We hid ourselves in the wood, and as we watched the boat near the island, we could see that there were ten men aboard and that they were well armed.

"I'm sure that three of the fellows I recognize were forced into mutiny," the captain said, peering at the boat, "but the boatswain and the rest were as guilty as everyone else aboard."

As he spoke, a worried expression crossed his face. "There are too many of them for us to overpower, surely?"

I smiled at him. "Why be afraid? When you came ashore you thought you were as good as dead anyway, so if you are to be killed, what have you lost?"

As to there being too many of them for us to overpower, they were ten, we were seven—me, Friday, the captain, the mate, the passenger, and two of the crew, who the captain had been convinced were telling the truth when they pledged loyalty to him.

Three of the others, black-hearted dogs according to the captain, had been taken to my fort, where Friday had tied and bound them but had left provisions for them and had promised that if they stayed quiet they would be freed within a day or so. But if they tried to escape, Friday assured them, they would be killed. The others, less enthusiastic mutineers according to the captain, had been similarly secured in my bower, as I believed it safer to split our captives into two separate parties.

When they saw the boat on the beach, the men nearing the island brought their own vessel as close to it as they could, waded ashore and hauled their boat onto dry land. This pleased me, for I had thought that they might have left their boat at anchor some distance from the shore, leaving men aboard to guard her.

The first thing they did was to run to the boat that was already there. From our vantage point within the woods fringing the beach, we could see and hear how surprised they were when they found her holed.

Then they shouted at the tops of their voices for their shipmates to come to the beach, and when their calls went unanswered, stood in a ring and fired their pistols into the air in a great volley that rang through the woods.

It was so loud that the men in the fort must have heard it, but so scared were they by Friday's threats that they gave no answering shout.

A minute or two later, the second group of men headed back to their boat. Later, they told us that they had intended to return to the ship, tell the crew that the men who had rowed the captain ashore had been murdered and then to set sail.

Fortunately they didn't. After a while, seven of the men came back to the shore, leaving three in the boat. This disappointed me, for if we overpowered the seven, the other three would certainly return to the ship. We watched the seven as they made their way along the beach and climbed the hill, calling for their comrades as they went.

"If they fire their pistols again," the captain whispered to me, "we could rush them as they reload."

"Good idea," I whispered.

But they didn't, and I was at a loss as to what to do.

Suddenly it came to me. I sent Friday and the mate to make their way to a small hill, close to the point where my servant had been brought ashore all those years ago.

"As soon as you get there," I said, "shout, and when the men shout back, move farther into the woods. Then shout again and again, each time drawing them farther and farther away from the beach and deep into the woods."

It looked as if I had left it too late, for the men started to make their way back to the boat. But just as they were about to get into it, I heard Friday's shout. The men aboard the boat brought it up the creek into a little natural harbour, and one of the three jumped off and joined the others as they ran along the beach answering Friday's call at the tops of their voices.

A few minutes later, Friday called again, this time his voice was slightly fainter. We watched the men getting smaller and smaller as Friday's calls drew them farther and farther away. The two left behind, one of whom the captain said had been lukewarm to the mutiny, were quickly overpowered.

That done, we pulled the boat out of the water and settled down in the woods to wait.

Chapter Sixteen

We Take the Ship

Night had fallen by the time Friday and the mate came back, followed some time later by the first of the crew. We watched them stagger along the beach in the moonlight, but long before they arrived, we heard them calling to each other, the ones behind shouting to those in front to wait for them as they were lame and tired.

When they came to the boat, run aground above the creek, we heard their cries of astonishment.

"This island is enchanted," cried one.

"Or haunted," cried another.

Suddenly they realized that their two shipmates were nowhere to be seen, and they began to call for them.

"Let's attack now," someone whispered in my ear.

"Best wait," I said. "We don't want to kill them all, and I don't want to risk any of our men getting shot. Let's see if they separate."

But when it became plain that they intended to stay close together, I told Friday and the captain to creep forward as close as they could without being seen and then to open fire.

But before they reached the fringe of the wood, the boatswain, the mutineers' ringleader, walked towards them with two others. My two men stood up and shot at the three men.

The boatswain fell dead almost immediately. One of the others fell to the ground, mortally wounded, although he did not die until several hours later. The third man ran for his life back to the others.

I, the captain and the rest of us rushed forward to join Friday, and we advanced on the body of the men.

Coming to them in the dark, the mutineers could not see how many we were. I told one of the men, now loyal to us, to call out to the mutineers, telling them to lay down their arms and surrender.

"Tom Smith," he called.

"Who's that? Robinson?" the man called Smith called back.

"Aye! Lay down your arms and yield or else you are all dead men."

"Who must we yield to? Where are they?"

"Here they are," called Robinson. "Here's our captain and fifty men who have been hunting you all these hours. The boatswain is dead, and Will Frye is injured. Yield or you'll be killed."

"Will you spare us?" shouted Smith.

"Do you recognize my voice?" called the captain.

"Aye!"

"Then tell your men to lay down their arms and you will all be spared. All except Will Atkins."

Atkins, the captain had told me, was the first man to lay a finger on him when the crew had mutinied and was the man who had threatened him with a cutlass on the beach when they had first arrived on the island.

"For pity's sake," cried Atkins, "spare me!"

"Lay down your arms and trust to the governor's mercy," the captain shouted, meaning that I was the governor.

"Very well," said Smith. "Throw down your arms, men."

When we were certain that the mutineers had truly surrendered, the captain went to talk to them while I decided to stay out of sight, for what governor would be dressed in goatskin.

I heard him tell the men that they had been mistaken in thinking the island had been uninhabited.

"It's governed by an Englishman," he said. "He could hang you, but he has given his word that you shall be spared as long as you are on his island. All except you, Atkins. You are to be hanged in the morning."

"What about the rest of us?" someone asked.

"You'll be sent back to England and dealt with there according to the law," said the captain.

From my hiding place, I saw Atkins fall to his knees and beg for his life. A moment later, the rest of them also knelt down, pleading not to be sent back to England, for they would certainly be hanged there for mutiny.

"We pledge ourselves to you," one of them said, at which there was a chorus of "Ayes".

"Captain," I called, "the governor calls you."

"Tell his excellency I am just coming," he replied, and turning to the men added, "Don't try anything. Remember you're surrounded by a force of fifty."

When he was by my side, I told the captain that with the number of men we now had, it should be an easy matter to retake the ship, but that first we must separate the real villains from the rest.

"Tell Friday that the governor commands him to take Will Atkins and one other of the worst of them to my fort and to tie them up with the others who are already there."

That done, I told my man to lead everyone else to my summer place and to hold them, along with those who had been taken there earlier, until the next morning.

When daylight came, I led the captain to the bower and stayed out of sight while he talked to them.

"If you help me retake my ship," I heard him say, "the governor has promised that he will recommend that you be pardoned when we return to England. If you don't, he will have you sent back on the next ship to be hanged in chains when you reach English territory!"

The men readily agreed, and we set to work repairing the holed boat.

It was some time later that two vessels left the beach heading for the ship. In the first were the captain, the mate and five men, and in the second, the passenger, whose name I forget and whom the captain put in charge, and four more men.

As to the others, those villains not held at my fort were kept on the island as hostages.

Friday and I also stayed behind to make sure that they caused no trouble.

I heard later how the captain and his men retook the ship.

As soon as they neared it, he made Robinson call out

and tell the men who were still aboard that they had brought everyone back from the island. When the two boats were at the ship's side, the captain and his mate scrambled aboard and, before anyone could stop them, hit the second mate and the ship's carpenter with the butt ends of their muskets. The rest of the men in the boats swarmed aboard, quickly overpowered the men on deck and locked the hatches to keep those below where they were.

Seeing what was happening, the new rebel captain locked himself in the roundhouse with two men and the ship's cabin boy. The door was quickly broken down, but when the mate and the captain burst in, the men inside fired, wounding the mate and two of the men outside.

Despite his wound, the mate fired at the would-be captain. The bullet entered the captain's mouth and came out again behind one of his ears, sending blood splattering in all directions. Seeing their leader killed, the men on deck surrendered, and a few minutes later, those below had been brought on deck and begged the captain for mercy.

As soon as the ship was his, the captain ordered that seven guns be fired—the signal of success that I was waiting for.

I was so exhausted that I lay down and slept and did not stir until I was wakened by a gunshot and the captain's voice calling, "Governor!"

"My dear friend and deliverer," he said when I was wide awake, "there's your ship, for she is all yours, and so are we that belong to her."

I looked out to sea and saw the vessel, about half a mile from the creek where I had first landed my rafts, and a few moments later I burst into tears.

When I had recovered my composure, the captain and I made our way to the beach where one of the ship's boats was anchored.

"Bring ashore the things I brought for the governor," he called.

His men brought me six large bottles of Madeira wine, two pounds of tobacco, twelve good pieces of ship's beef, six pieces of port, a bag full of lemons and a bottle of lime cordial.

Even better, he gave me six new shirts, two pairs of gloves, a pair of shoes, a fine hat, a pair of stockings and a suit of his own clothes, which fitted me perfectly.

It was a very agreeable present, as one may imagine, to one in my circumstances, but I found it strange to put on decent clothes for the first time.

"You look every inch the governor now," the captain said when I stood before him, fully dressed.

I smiled and bowed to him, and as I did so, a thought struck me. "What," I said, "shall we do with the prisoners in my fort?"

"They are such villains that if we take them aboard they must be held in irons and handed over to the authorities at the first English colony we come to," said the captain.

"No doubt they'll be hanged," I said.

"No doubt." The captain's voice was sad, for he was a kind-hearted fellow.

"How would it be if I persuaded them all to stay on the island?"

When the captain agreed, I told him to go back to his ship and hang the body of the dead usurper from the yardarm and to bring the ship closer into shore.

I waited until that was done before asking Friday to bring the prisoners from the fort to me.

When they were before me, I pointed to the ship.

"Your captain has taken the ship, and you can see how he has rewarded the man who took his place."

They looked horrified when they saw the body dangling from the yardarm.

"Is there any reason why you should not hang too?" I asked.

When no-one answered, I told them that I was going to leave the island with all my men—for they still believed there were fifty of us—and that if we were to take them with us, the captain would be obliged to keep them in chains all the way to England where they would be hanged for their mutiny.

"As for me," I went on, "I have a mind to leave you here. If you learn the ways of the island, you may well survive. It is," I went on, "your only chance of life."

After the men had agreed, I asked the captain and the rest of the men to return to the ship and to come back for me in the morning.

"I'm in no danger from them," I said, nodding at the prisoners. "They won't dare harm me."

When the captain and the others had gone, I told those to be left behind my true story—that I was no governor but a shipwrecked sailor who had been on the island for many years. I showed them where my bower was, told them how to plant corn and harvest it, how to make bread and how to dry grapes.

I took them to my flock of goats and instructed them as to how to milk the beasts and make butter and cheese.

And when it was time for me to go to the ship, I gave them firearms, powder and shot.

Just before I left, I told them to expect the Spaniards whom the Spaniard and Friday's father had gone to collect from the mainland.

By the time I got to the ship, we had missed the tide and so spent the night at anchor.

Just as we were about to set sail the next morning, two of the men we had left behind swam out to the ship and pleaded to be taken aboard.

"The others will murder us if we stay there," they spluttered.

The captain agreed to take them with us, and, as soon as they were on board, had them whipped so soundly that they behaved perfectly all the way home.

Friday and I stood on deck and watched the island getting smaller and smaller as we sailed away from it. All I had with me, apart from my new clothes, were my large goatskin cap, my umbrella, Poll my parrot, and the £36 I had found on my ship as I stripped her of everything I could so long before.

And so it was that on the 19th day of December, 1686, having been on the island for twenty-eight years, two months and nineteen days, I left it behind, and by the time we reached England I had been away for thirty-five years.

Glossary

The words and phrases in the glossary that follows have been chosen to help the reader understand their meaning in the specific context of this book (although sometimes they may have other additional meanings). Many of the words and phrases pertain to the more formal language of the seventeenth and eighteenth centuries and are no longer in regular use today.

We recommend you also use a dictionary when reading this book.

abated died down, became less

ahoy a shout used to attract attention, especially in boats

alongside along the side of or next to, as in: "as they came alongside (our ship), we were unable to stop them swarming aboard"

apiece each

apprehensions fears or anxieties about what may happen

as calm as a millpond very calm and still

bag(ged) to capture or kill game (wild birds and animals)

barter to trade goods without money

baubles and trinkets small ornaments or items of jewellery that are of little value

bear down on someone to move quickly towards someone in a threatening way

becalmed motionless because there is no wind (of a sailing ship)

boatswain (pronounced **boe**-sun) the officer on a ship who is responsible for the maintenance of the ship and its equipment

bow of a ship the front part of a ship

bower a shady, leafy shelter

breeches trousers (sometimes extending to the knee or just below) worn for riding or mountaineering

broadside facing sideways, as in: "trying to catch them broadside"

burned at the stake executed by being tied to a post and burned alive

call of the sea the strong attraction or appeal of a life on board ship

caught the fever infected with any one of various diseases in which a high temperature is present

coursing racing, moving swiftly

devoured swallowed or eaten up greedily

distress flare a device for producing a blaze of light to signal that help is needed

every man jack every single person in a group

false dawn a promising situation that comes to nothing or something that seems to show a situation is improving when it is not

flood (**the tide**) to start coming in or rising

fogbound prevented from moving because of thick fog

following wind a wind blowing in the same direction that a ship is taking

forecastle (pronounced **foke**-sul) the section of the upper deck of a ship that is at the front end of the ship

fortify to strengthen and make safe

fowling pistol/fowling piece a gun used to shoot wild birds

fresh wind a wind that is brisk, quite strong and often cool

fringe on the edge of something or the less important parts of something

get your tongue around to pronounce a difficult word correctly

go into trade to start working in the field of business or commerce

grave dignified or serious and sad

hammock a length of canvas or net hung between two trees or other supports and used as a bed

have no head for to have no natural ability to do something

holed with a hole in it

hug the coast to keep very close to the coast

Land ahoy! an exclamation made by a sailor whose job it is to inform the crew that land has been seen

larder a place where food is stored or a supply of food

lightship a moored or anchored ship equipped with lights to warn or guide ships at sea

lustily loudly and with great enjoyment

makeshift suitable as a substitute or replacement for a short time

Maresco of Islamic, Spanish and northwest African descent

marauding wandering in search of victims or things to steal

mate an officer on a merchant ship/cargo ship ranking next below the master/captain of the ship

millpond a pond for supplying water to a mill wheel

Moor a member of a traditionally Muslim people

musket an old type of gun

mutiny the open rebellion of sailors against their officers

nanny goat female goat

natives indigenous people (when used in reference to members of an indigenous people, the noun "native", like its synonym "aborigine", is considered dated and offensive)

needlessly in a way that is not necessary

of desperate fortune whose position in life was really bad

on the brink of starvation just about to starve to death

pickings a group of things that may be taken (from the ship)

pieces of eight old Spanish silver coins (also known as a Spanish dollars or eight-real coins)

plain a level or almost level piece of land, especially one with no trees

planter/plantationer the owner or manager of a plantation (a large estate or farm, especially in tropical countries, whose workforce historically consisted of slaves from Africa)

pondering thinking over something deeply and seriously

Portuguese caravel a small sailing ship whose economy, speed, agility and power made it one of the best sailing vessels of its time

purchase to buy

recant to formally withdraw or take back an earlier belief or statement

reckon with to deal with

ringleader a person who leads others in any kind of unlawful activity or informal activity

run aground when a ship has hit rocks or a reef or a sandbar in shallow water off the coast, as a result of which it often sinks. The ship is often broken into bits

Sallee (Salé) a city in northwestern Morocco that was once an independent republic and a haven for pirates (in the time before it was incorporated into Morocco)

salt in my veins having a deep love for life on board ship

savages members of an uncivilized and primitive people (this usage is chiefly found in historical or literary contexts and is considered offensive nowadays—it is not acceptable to use this term to describe indigenous peoples)

scrub sparse, stunted vegetation

scrubland land covered in scrub

scudded moved along quickly and smoothly

sea shanties songs sung by sailors

shot tiny lead or steel pellets or balls fired from a gun

slung thrown or flung

squall a brief, sudden and violent windstorm (especially at sea)

stricken broken, disabled

swigged took a great gulp of

tallow a hard fat obtained from the bodies of sheep/goats/cattle that is used to make candles

taper a long, wax-coated wick to light a candle

throw up to vomit

timbers the wooden support frames of a ship

tot a small measure or amount (especially of an alcoholic drink)

transatlantic crossing the Atlantic Ocean, on or from the other side of the Atlantic

turn a deaf ear to choose to refuse to listen or hear something

venture something we choose to do that is risky or

dangerous (such as go on a journey)

vittle food or provisions for human beings

volley the firing of several weapons at the same time

watch the officers and crew on duty in a ship

what he would have me do what he wanted me to do

whim a sudden wish or urge to do something for no particular reason

world was at my feet I felt that I could successfully take on all the things the world had to offer

yard a long, tapering wooden pole attached to a mast to support and spread out a square sail

yardarm either end of the two ends of a ship's yard (see above)

yield to give in (to someone's request or demand)